BEDS

BEDS

*Outstanding Projects from
One of America's Best Craftsmen*

WITH PLANS AND COMPLETE INSTRUCTIONS
FOR BUILDING 9 CLASSIC BEDS

JEFF MILLER

The Taunton Press

Publisher: Jim Childs
Associate publisher: Helen Albert
Associate editor: Strother Purdy
Copy editor: Nancy N. Bailey
Indexer: Peter Chapman
Cover designer: Steve Hughes
Interior designer: Lori Wendin
Layout artists: Lori Wendin and Amy Bernard Russo
Front cover photographer: Randy O'Rourke
Back cover photographer: Tanya Tucka
Interior photographer: Tanya Tucka, except where noted
Illustrator: Bob La Pointe

Taunton
BOOKS & VIDEOS
for fellow enthusiasts

Printed in the United States of America
10 9 8 7 6 5 4 3 2 1

The Taunton Press, Inc.,
63 South Main Street, PO Box 5506, Newtown, CT 06470-5506
e-mail: tp@taunton.com

Distributed by Publishers Group West

Library of Congress Cataloging-in-Publication Data
Miller, Jeff, 1956-
    Beds: outstanding projects from one of America's best craftsmen / Jeff Miller.
        p.   cm. — (Step-by-step)
    ISBN 1-56158-254-9
    1. Beds. 2. Furniture making. I. Title. II. Series: Step-by-Step (Taunton Press)
TT197.5.B4M55   1999
684.1'5 dc21   99-15009
                                                                         CIP

ABOUT YOUR SAFETY

Working with wood is inherently dangerous. Using hand or power tools improperly or ignoring standard safety practices can lead to permanent injury or even death. Don't try to perform operations you learn about here (or elsewhere) unless you're certain they are safe for you. If something about an operation doesn't feel right, don't do it. Look for another way. We want you to enjoy the craft, so please keep safety foremost in your mind whenever you're working with wood.

To Becky, Isaac, and Ariel

ACKNOWLEDGMENTS

A book like this isn't written without help. Some of the help—a quick check of a fact or the confirmation of the sanity of an idea—is casual, the stuff of friendship. I thank all of those who've assisted me in this way for their support. Other help is much more substantial. Around the shop, I've gotten help, support, and friendship through both ordinary times and some rather extraordinary ones from Bruce Sharp, Craig Klucina, Andy Brownell, Jason Holtz, Bruce McDonald, and Tracy Perrizo. Tanya Tucka's willingness to run over to photograph whatever was going on—making it look not only easy but good as well—made the process ever so much easier. I value the help I've gotten from Strother Purdy, Helen Albert, and Nancy Bailey at Taunton, especially Strother's willingness to put up with my questions, opinions, and rantings.

A special thanks to Birgitte Williams, who allowed me to set up shop in her basement so many years ago, getting me started down this fascinating path.

And I always carry with me the support of my parents, my wife, and my children.

CONTENTS

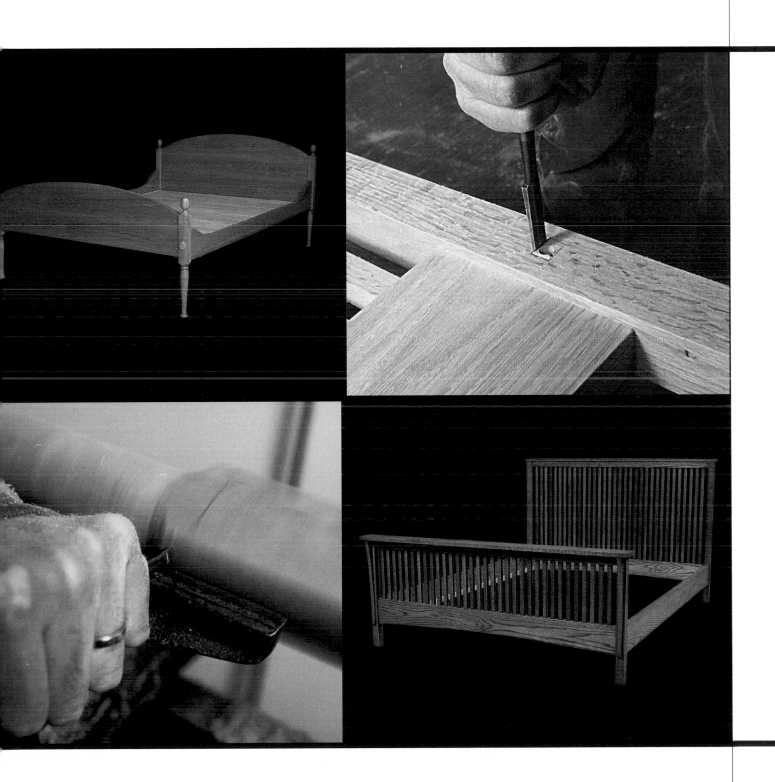

INTRODUCTION

We spend close to a third of our lives in bed. For this reason alone, in an increasingly fast-paced and sleep-deprived world, our beds are our most important place of repose. But it is the other activities that help make our beds so special. We watch television. We read stories to our children. We stay up too late ourselves with a good book (a pleasure usually regretted the next day). Our children use the bed as a trampoline. We use the bed as a…trampoline. And we serve breakfast in bed as a very special treat.

For these reasons, the bed is one of the most significant pieces of furniture in the home, ranking with the dining room table as a major purchase or project. But where the dining table is something of a showpiece, the bed has a more private meaning. Our choice of bed reveals more of our innermost ideas of repose, comfort, and family life. Physical comfort is not the issue—that's up to the mattress. It's the bed frame that matters. In building or choosing one, it's almost as if we're creating some sort of private shelter. This intimate shelter can take many forms—from the pure and simple to the rich and imposing.

Whatever the bed looks like—austere or elaborate—the basic structure is fairly simple. The headboard and footboard are generally separate pieces connected to the side rails with some form of knockdown joinery. There are more complex variations, but I haven't found much use for them. I've developed a quick, easy, and very sturdy connection system based on traditional bed bolts, which I use on most of the projects in this book.

This book can be seen as a collection of good bed projects that utilize this simple system. Where appropriate, I've given options for changing some of the designs to serve as variations or further projects. But this book is more than just projects. The bed designs cover a wide range of woodworking techniques and can lead to the mastery of an equally wide range of woodworking skills. Tapering long posts, laminating big curves, cutting and smoothing graceful shapes, even creating large round posts—all are a part of the standard repertoire of the bed maker and cabinetmaker.

In the first chapter, I walk you through the basics of building beds. What follows are nine bed projects. You can pick a project based on good design fundamentals that can expand your woodworking capabilities. Or you can use these basic designs as a foundation from which to design your own bed.

Bed-Building Basics

BEDS COME IN all shapes, sizes, and kinds. There are dozens of basic forms, hundreds of different styles, and thousands of variations. However, the only essential part of a bed is what we actually lie down and sleep on. This usually means a mattress in one form or another. In fact, the word "bed" was originally used to describe just the bedding; the word "bedstead" applied to the other parts of what we now think of as a bed. With all of this variety, it's surprising how similar the basic construction of most beds is.

Basic Bed Components

A typical bed has a headboard, footboard, side rails, and some sort of mattress support. Not all beds have all these parts—some are little more than the mattress, while others add on all sorts of extras. But whatever the bed consists of, there is one almost universal feature: knockdown joinery. This is simply a matter of practicality. A bed is just too hard to move around as a single unit, so each component is indeed a separate part. We'll consider each of the parts separately before we look at how to put them together.

The headboard

The headboard is usually the visual focus of the bed. It establishes the look and the style and is generally the most ornate part. It's a good place to show off your skills as a woodworker, as long as the design is well integrated throughout the rest of the bed.

On a typical wooden bed, the headboard consists of the two legs (or posts) at the head of the bed, the headboard rail, and some sort of a board that extends up above the mattress. The term *headboard* is sometimes used to describe just this board; at other times it describes the complete headboard assembly, including the legs, rails, and, of course, this headboard plank. I will use *headboard* to describe the assembly and *headboard plank* to describe the plank.

Functionally, the headboard keeps the pillows from slipping off the bed and the wall from getting dirty from contact with heads and hair oils. On the other hand, the headboard doesn't always end up against the wall. Some people place the bed in the middle of the room. The nineteenth-century writer Mark Twain placed the footboard of his antique Italian bed against the wall. With pillows against the footboard, he could look at the beautifully ornate headboard down by his feet when in bed. Most people are not quite this eccentric.

Headboard heights can vary from just higher than the pillow to many feet higher than the mattress. This is mostly a matter of style and design, although a low headboard makes it easy to knock your head if you toss and turn at night. I recommend a minimum height of 10 in. to 12 in. above the mattress.

Parts of a Bed

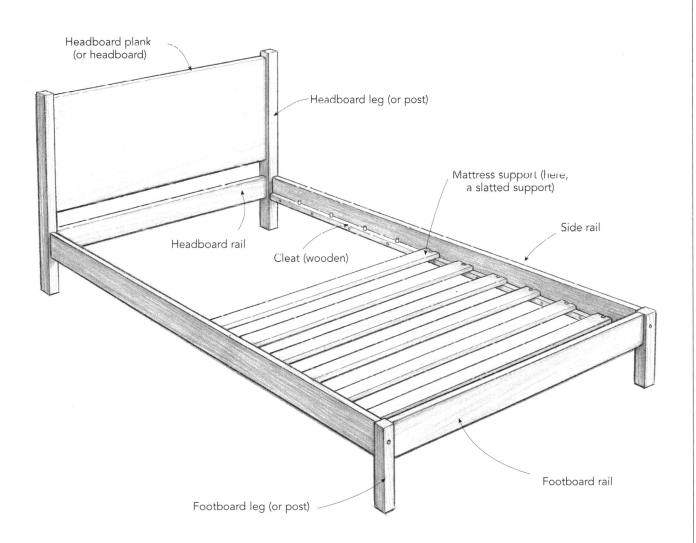

Headboard plank (or headboard)

Headboard leg (or post)

Mattress support (here, a slatted support)

Side rail

Headboard rail

Cleat (wooden)

Footboard rail

Footboard leg (or post)

The footboard

The footboard is often a scaled-down version of the headboard, reflecting and complementing the headboard's elements. It can be as complex as the headboard or as simple as two legs and a connecting rail.

The footboard can be simple because it doesn't have as important a function as the headboard. Originally it may have helped to keep the mattress in place. Now it's mostly a design convention that adds visual balance to the bed.

Some people don't like the confinement of a footboard. Some don't like the fact that it makes dealing with sheets and blankets a little more difficult. Others find the visual and physical closure at the bottom of the bed comforting. Choosing a footboard design really comes down to personal preference. When you make a similar headboard and footboard, build both at once, so that you need to set up machines and jigs only once for work on both.

The side rails

There usually isn't a whole lot to the side rails, beyond holding everything together. On most beds, they are simply rectangular boards. One reason that the side rails don't get all that much attention is that the sheets and/or blankets will often cover them. However, there are plenty of ways to dress them up. Especially on beds with curves, the side rails can echo and complement the design.

Structurally, the side rails connect the headboard and the footboard and support the mattress. This is accomplished most often with some sort of knockdown hardware so the bed doesn't have to be moved in one piece.

METAL FRAMES & WOODEN HEADBOARDS

It's fairly common to see a bed with a wooden headboard attached to a metal bed frame. Some metal frames come with a bracket for this purpose. You screw the bracket to the headboard (or bolt into a threaded insert in the leg), then slide it onto the pins on the frame.

These kinds of beds are much easier to make, but the connection between a metal bed frame and a wooden headboard is usually quite wobbly. The metal frame is not designed well for this purpose, and the connection is too low to hold the headboard securely. Instead, you could try attaching the headboard directly to the wall.

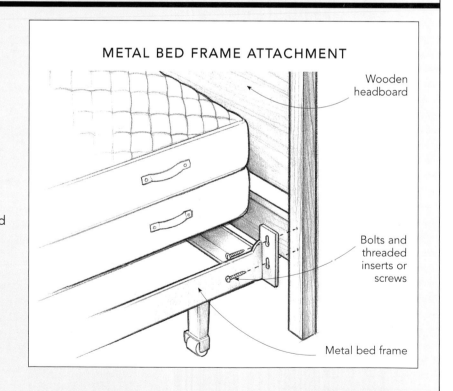

METAL BED FRAME ATTACHMENT

Wooden headboard

Bolts and threaded inserts or screws

Metal bed frame

Box-Spring Supports

Box springs have a rigid frame and so need support only along the edges.

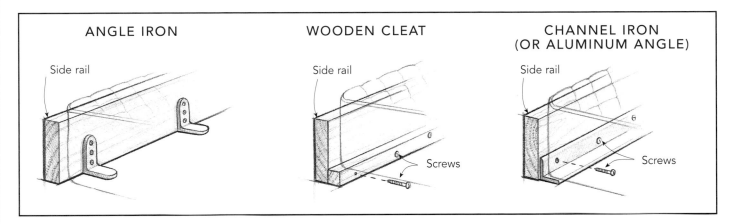

ANGLE IRON — Side rail

WOODEN CLEAT — Side rail, Screws

CHANNEL IRON (OR ALUMINUM ANGLE) — Side rail, Screws

KING-SIZE BED

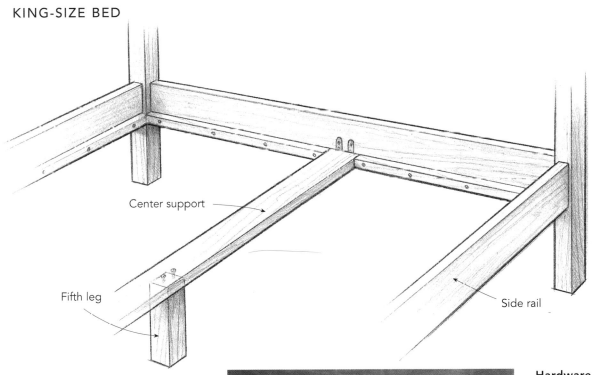

Center support

Fifth leg

Side rail

A king-size bed needs a center support to support either the middle of the two-piece box spring or the long span of the slats.

Hardware designed for the center support on a king-size bed makes setting up and knocking down the bed easy. Simple angle brackets also function well.

MATTRESS SUPPORTS

The last major component of a bed is something to support the mattress. This can be either a box spring—a wooden frame containing springs—or a platform foundation.

Box-spring supports

Many beds have a box spring as well as a mattress. According to the International Sleep Products Association (ISPA), a box spring is sold along with about 80 percent of the mattresses in this country. Box springs are designed as a semi-rigid support. They can absorb some of the impact of a person sitting, lying, or even jumping on a bed, which prolongs the life of the mattress. Many people find the springy support of a box spring more comfortable than wooden mattress supports.

From a bed builder's viewpoint, it is easier to build a wooden frame bed for a box spring. While a simple mattress needs slats or a platform to support it, a box spring is supported around the edges. On all but a king-size bed, a simple wooden cleat or even a series of mattress hanger irons screwed in place around the inside of the bed rails is enough. On a king-size bed, which uses two twin-size box springs side by side as the foundation, you need a support running from headboard to footboard down the middle of the bed and a fifth leg in the middle of this support.

For years, I just attached this center support with small angle brackets. This functioned well but had to be screwed into place when setting up the bed. Now there is a specific piece of knockdown hardware available just for this purpose. It's a little harder to install in the shop than the angle brackets, but when setting up the bed, you can just drop the support into place.

Platform foundations

The alternative to the box spring is the platform foundation, which can support mattresses without a box spring. There are two common types of platform support: slatted and solid, which is made with plywood (or similar sheet material). In Europe, slatted foundations, often using laminated slats instead of solid wood ones, are very common. In this country, the term *platform bed* usually means a plywood support surface.

I much prefer slats for mattress support. Slats have some give and so act like wooden springs with each slat moving and flexing independently of the others. This makes for firmer support than a box spring, but one that is still flexible. Although individual slats may not look strong enough to support people

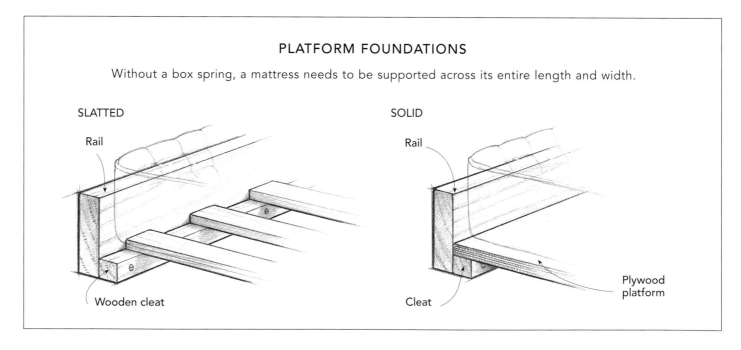

PLATFORM FOUNDATIONS

Without a box spring, a mattress needs to be supported across its entire length and width.

SLATTED

Rail

Wooden cleat

SOLID

Rail

Cleat

Plywood platform

without breaking, once weight is distributed across them, they hold up very well and their support is quite good. Slats also allow the mattress to "breathe" through the spaces, for whatever that's worth.

Slats are a bit more work to make than a simple plywood platform. They also will move around over time, leaving parts of the mattress unsupported, unless you provide some form of alignment or attachment. Slats are also better at a different kind of moving around: They are very portable, especially if they're piled together and strapped into two bundles, which are much easier to move than either a box spring or a sheet of plywood.

A plywood platform has its own advantages and disadvantages. A plywood platform is less trouble to make; but without significant support underneath, even a ¾-in.-thick plywood platform will sag. Unlike the slats, the entire piece of plywood tends to sag as a unit. Sagging plywood is definitely not comfortable to sleep on because your spine will match the sag. However, a recessed box resting on the floor can easily support a platform on all bed sizes except the king. There, you can add additional structure inside the box. You can also use wooden or metal struts underneath to support a platform without a box.

A well-supported plywood platform is fine to sleep on, although still firmer than a slatted platform. Ultimately, this added firmness can shorten the life of a mattress, unless the mattress is specifically designed for platform use.

A very different support problem is created by waterbed mattresses. These should have plywood platforms, but they must be reinforced with a more extensive grid structure underneath to help distribute the weight of the water over a greater area of the floor. Almost any bed design can be turned into a waterbed by adding a support grid underneath the platform. There are commercially available metal frames that do the same thing.

SIZING A BED

To the sleeper, the most important part of the bed is the mattress. If the bed and platform are structurally sound, the mattress deter-

This grid inside of a box is one way to distribute the weight of a waterbed mattress over a larger area. A diagonal grid is also a possibility.

mines the comfort of the bed. To the woodworker, however, none of this is of much interest. The most important thing a woodworker needs to know about a mattress is its size, and this is a big deal indeed.

Mattresses vary in size more than enough to cause big problems for the woodworker. The standard mattress sizes I've encountered are listed in the chart on p. 10. I use them as a rule of thumb because variations in size are quite common. I've come across mattresses that were as much as 1 in. wider or narrower than standard. The lesson here is that it's very important that you measure the length and the width of the mattress you'll be using with the bed. But don't make a wooden bed to fit a slightly undersized mattress because a bed should outlast any particular mattress. It could become difficult later on to find another undersized mattress.

Mattress thicknesses vary far more than their width and length—up to 9 in. Many mattresses are still made roughly 6 in. to 7 in. thick. But the trend in the industry is to make thicker and thicker mattresses. Some can be around 14 in. or 15 in. thick. This can really cause problems on a bed designed for a 6-in.-to 7-in.-thick mattress by covering all or most of a headboard and footboard. If you want to use a thick mattress, adjust the proportions of the bed to accommodate the added bulk.

Mattress Thickness and Bed Proportions

Matresses can vary by up to 9" in thickness. Design headboards and footboards to accommodate the actual thickness of the mattress you will use.

STANDARD BED SIZES		
Standard Name	Width (in.)	Length (in.)
Twin	39	75
Double or full	54	75
Queen	60	80
King	76	80
California king	72	84

The mattress visually overwhelms this bed.

The same mattress fits this bed, which has a taller headboard and footboard.

Determining correct headboard and footboard rail lengths

It's easy enough to know you want the distance between side rails to be about ⅛ in. to ¼ in. greater than the mattress is wide. It's another matter, however, to translate that measurement into the exact length of the headboard and footboard rails. This length depends on a combination of the space between the rails, the width of the legs, and the side rail thickness. A scale or full-size drawing will do the job. But I've devised two formulas described in "Determining Rail Lengths."

BED HARDWARE

The real trick to bed building is putting all of these parts together. And you have to do it in a way that is very rigid and durable when the bed is together but still easy to take apart for moving or storage. There are many ways to address this problem but few that really solve it well.

Bed bolts

The best solution that I've found is still a compromise: bed bolts. I rely on these in one form or another on almost all of my beds. No other fastener has the same reliability. The joint is very solid over long periods of time and can be easily tightened if necessary. There are drawbacks, however. It's not the easiest way to assemble a bed. You have to have the necessary wrench in order to set up or disassemble the bed, and you have to keep track of both the wrench and the bolts when the bed is moved or stored. And bed bolts usually require holes in the outside faces of the legs—some people find the holes visually distracting.

Bed bolts come in several styles. You can still buy the traditional-style iron bed bolt, some form of which has been used in beds for centuries. These bolts have a square head, a wide flange to seat securely against the bottom of the hole into which they're recessed, and a pointed end to help thread easily into the nut that is embedded in the rail. They also require a special bed bolt wrench. Many woodworking and specialty period hardware catalogs carry both the bolts and the wrenches.

You can also use simple hex-head bolts with nuts and washers from a hardware store. These are convenient to buy and a little easier to use because you don't have to embed the nuts carefully into the rails.

DETERMINING RAIL LENGTHS

These two formulas may look a little intimidating, but they're actually quite simple once you know what all the letters mean. Only simple math is required.

$$L = W - (x - y) + (t \times 2)$$

To translate this into English, we want to figure out the length of the headboard or footboard rail, which we'll call L. We know the width of the mattress. Adding $\frac{1}{8}$ in. to $\frac{1}{4}$ in. to that width gives us W, the distance we want between the side rails.

Next we need to know the distance between the side rails and the inside face of the leg. If the side rail is centered in the leg, then this distance is equal to the thickness of the leg X minus the thickness of the rail Y divided by two. As this measurement needs to be subtracted from both ends, we just use X-Y (subtracting (X-Y)/2 twice is the same as subtracting X-Y). At this point, you have the distance between tenon shoulders. Add the two tenon lengths T for an overall rail length.

On a bed where the legs or rails may be different sizes, you'll need this formula:

$$L = W - \frac{X1-Y1}{2} - \frac{X2-Y2}{2} + T1 + T2$$

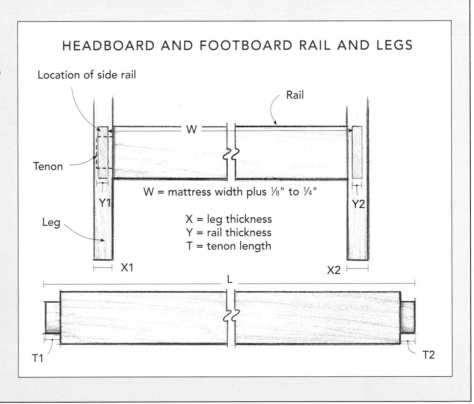

HEADBOARD AND FOOTBOARD RAIL AND LEGS

Location of side rail

Rail

Tenon

W

Leg

W = mattress width plus $\frac{1}{8}$" to $\frac{1}{4}$"

X = leg thickness
Y = rail thickness
T = tenon length

Y1

Y2

X1

X2

L

T1

T2

Bed Bolt Joints

TRADITIONAL BOLT JOINT

Bed bolts join side rails to bed posts with great stength.

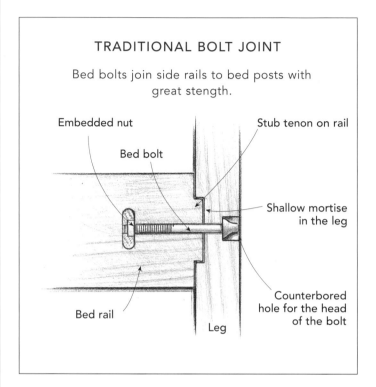

Embedded nut

Bed bolt

Stub tenon on rail

Shallow mortise in the leg

Counterbored hole for the head of the bolt

Bed rail

Leg

Bed bolt joints need a way to prevent the parts from twisting. A shallow mortise-and-tenon joint works perfectly.

HEX-HEAD BOLT JOINT

This works as well as traditional bed bolts. The hardware is commonly available.

D-shaped recess on inside of rail

Nut

5/16" diameter dowel

Counterbored hole for head of bolt and washer

Washer

5/16" hex-head bolt

Bed rail

Leg

Dowels are an alternative to the shallow mortise and tenon and are shown here with a hex-head bolt joint.

BARREL NUT JOINT

Barrel nuts differ only in the shape of the nut and the nut recess. They require thicker rails than the other types of bed bolts.

Flat-bottomed hole on inside of rail

Barrel nut

5/16" dowel

Counterbored hole for head of bolt and washer

3/8" bolt

Washer

Bed rail

Leg

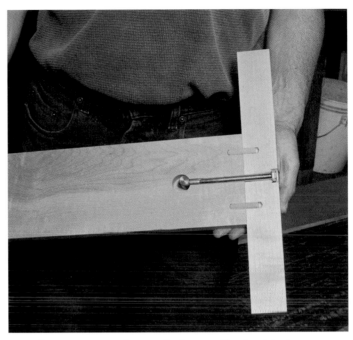

Barrel nuts are another variation on the bed bolt.

HIDDEN BOLT JOINT

It is possible to reverse the orientation of bed bolts and not have a hole on the outside face of the leg.

T-shaped recess on inside of rail

5/16" bolt

Washer

5/16" diameter dowel

Tenon from headboard or footboard rail

5/16" square nut embedded in outer cheek of the tenon

Bed rail

Leg

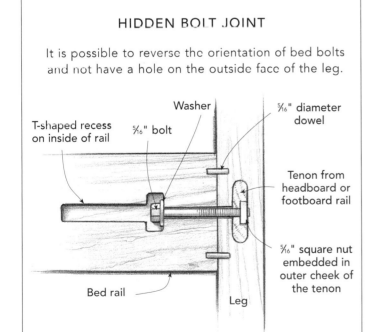

Bed bolts can be hidden by reversing their orientation so that they screw in from the rail into the leg. This requires some ingenuity and a fair bit more work.

They are slightly harder to work with during assembly, however, with the loose washers and nuts.

To solve the problem of safe storage of the less common assembly tool, I've also used socket-head bolts, which need an Allen wrench to tighten. You can easily make a notch for the Allen wrench on one of the side rail cleats, so it's always available. However, long socket head bolts are not easy to find.

Using bed bolts

Whatever type of bed bolt you use, it will not make a complete joint by itself. It holds the rail tightly against the leg but doesn't prevent the rail from rotating or shifting up, down, or side to side. Bed bolts must be used in con-junction with a locating system that prevents this motion and ensures proper alignment.

On traditional beds, a very short tenon on the end of the rail is the most common solution. This tenon plugs into a shallow mortise on the leg that should be only about 1/4 in. to 1/2 in. deep to avoid weakening the leg (see the top drawing on p. 12). The bolt runs through the middle of the mortise-and-tenon joint and secures it.

An alternative is to use two 5/16-in.-diameter dowels, one on either side of the bolt. They are not necessarily as strong as a mortise-and-tenon joint, but they're still more than strong enough. Don't forget that the bolt and nut hold the joint together. The mortise and tenon or the dowel is not glued.

HIDING THE BED BOLT HOLES

The easiest way to use a bed bolt leaves a hole on the outside face of a leg. You can leave the holes exposed or conceal them with decorative covers. Commercial metal covers usually pivot on the screw on which they hang; some are simple wooden mushroom plugs. Though the wooden plugs look fine, they tend to fall out and get lost over time. You can also make custom wooden covers in any shape or style you want.

Truth be told, I don't mind the holes that much. I tend to think of them the way I think of the scribed layout lines in a hand-cut dovetail joint. They are a sign of quality and a reflection of the way the piece is put together. Not everyone agrees with me on this, however.

Top left: Bed bolt covers swivel on a single screw, effectively hiding the bed bolt hole, but allowing easy access.

Top right: Bed bolt covers come in a surprisingly wide variety of styles. Some are made from stamped sheet brass, but the higher quality ones are cast brass.

Left: The wooden mushroom plug is another easy way to conceal a bolt hole.

Barrel nuts

A simple variation of the bed bolt and nut is the bolt and barrel nut. The only difference is in the nut, which is a section of metal rod with a threaded hole running through it crosswise. This makes it a little easier to install the nut: You just drill a hole. However, this works better in concept than in reality. Barrel nuts impose limitations that typical bolts and nuts don't. For example, they only work on rails that are at least 1⁵/₁₆ in. thick. Plus there is a need for either considerable accuracy or a fair amount of fussing to get the nuts to work properly.

Hidden bolts

There are ways to use bed bolts without leaving holes on the outside of the leg. You just switch the orientation of the bolt and nut so that the nut is embedded in the leg and the bolt is inserted through a T-shaped recess on the inside face of the side rail. The wide part of the recess allows you to tighten the bolt once it is fully in its hole. You'll find this variation on the Craftsman-Style Bed on p. 90, the Platform Bed on p. 130, and the Sleigh Bed on p. 144.

Other bed assembly hardware

There are many other types of commercial mechanical fasteners available for assembling

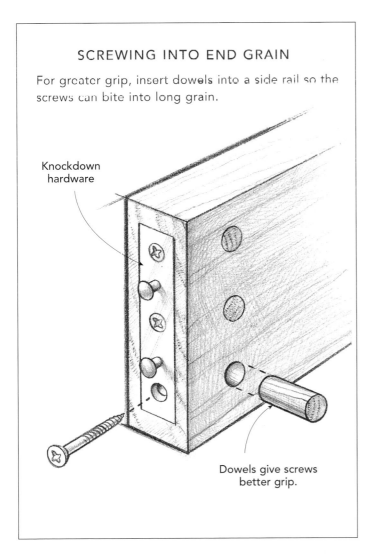

SCREWING INTO END GRAIN

For greater grip, insert dowels into a side rail so the screws can bite into long grain.

Knockdown hardware

Dowels give screws better grip.

Here are a few of the many bed rail fasteners out on the market: hooks, sliding keys, cams, and other interlocking mechanisms.

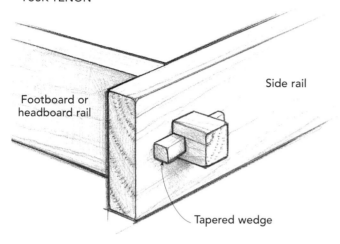

beds, incorporating various kinds of hooks, wedges, cams, and screws. The attraction of most of these is that they are invisible from the outside of the bed. Most are quite convenient because they don't require tools to assemble the bed—you just slip one part into the other and push down. Unfortunately, most of them fail to make a joint that is either rigid enough or durable enough over time.

There are a few things to consider when judging the potential of a particular fastener. First, do you have to screw into end grain to attach the fastener to the bed rail? This is a potentially serious problem since screws will eventually pull out of end grain. To help solve this problem, you can drill holes in the rail and insert dowels perpendicular to the screw hole. This way the screws will pass through the long grain of the dowels.

Next, is the hardware itself well made? Look for the sturdiest hardware you can find. Does it incorporate some form of a wedge to tighten the joint fully? The wedging action that comes from a tapered prong or hook allows you to tighten the joint simply by tapping down on the rail if it loosens over time.

If the hardware passes these tests, I like to try out the fastener in a mock-up joint to see if it's easy to install and use, if there are any unusual dimensional requirements, and if it makes a rigid enough connection. Unfortunately, I haven't found any perfect solutions—at least not yet.

WOODEN KNOCKDOWN JOINTS

There are ways to make a bed using wooden knockdown joints, too. These are not very common, but they can make solid connections and interesting additions to bed designs. There is a common problem with these joints: one part (either the side rail or the headboard or footboard rail) needs to protrude out from the bed edge so that there is enough wood for a solid joint. This can be brutal on shins. You can train yourself to walk around, but I still have scars from my "training period." I don't use these joints any more.

An Under-Bed Storage Box on Wheels

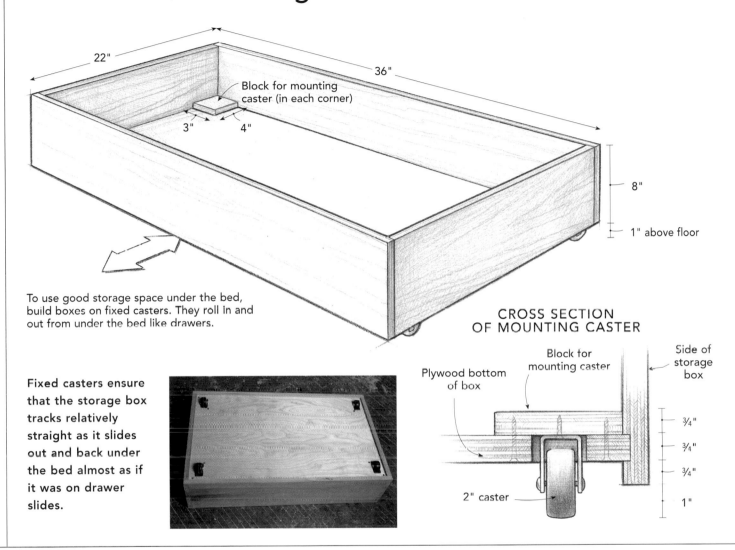

22"

36"

Block for mounting caster (in each corner)

3"   4"

8"

1" above floor

To use good storage space under the bed, build boxes on fixed casters. They roll in and out from under the bed like drawers.

CROSS SECTION OF MOUNTING CASTER

Plywood bottom of box

Block for mounting caster

Side of storage box

¾"

¾"

¾"

1"

2" caster

Fixed casters ensure that the storage box tracks relatively straight as it slides out and back under the bed almost as if it was on drawer slides.

STORAGE UNDER THE BED

Under-the-bed storage is a great way to use a large and otherwise wasted space. After experimenting with all kinds of methods for hanging drawers off the bed frame, I've decided that having a drawer box roll on the ground works best. My design is very straightforward. It's just a box with casters set into the bottom. I use rubber-wheel casters—the fixed kind, not the swiveling ones—and the box pulls out

almost straight as if it was on drawer slides. You can pull the box (or boxes) all the way out from under the bed, which is a big advantage over drawers mounted to the frame.

There are other, less complicated ways to make the storage box roll. You can get very low profile casters and also special bed box wheels that screw to the outside of the box. But I like the feel of the 2-in. rubber-wheel casters, and they roll well on most surfaces, though I wouldn't go so far as to include shag carpeting.

First Bed

This bed is basic, unadorned, and simple. It's an ideal first bed project because its very simplicity also makes it perfect as an introduction to making any other bed. We examine all of the basic elements of making a typical wooden bed in this chapter. We use some variation of these methods on all of the beds in this book—except for the Platform Bed, which has a different structure entirely—so this project also functions as an overall reference.

This "first" bed has a simple headboard, but no real footboard—just legs and a footboard rail. The bed sets up and disassembles easily using bolts with washers and nuts. The side rails support a series of wooden slats, which create the platform to hold the mattress. The whole thing is easy to store or move around, since the parts are reasonably small and relatively light.

This bed is also a first bed in another way—it's a good first bed for a child because it's a little lower than usual. But it certainly doesn't have to be this way. You could add 2 in. to the legs to bring the rails up to 10 in. off the floor, making it a more typical adult bed. I give the basic dimensions for the other standard sizes as well, since all of the techniques and approaches described here apply to any size bed; just the dimensions need to be recalculated.

Simple First Bed for a Child or Adult

THE FIRST BED is quite simple and introduces the basic structure of a wooden bed. The headboard and footboard rails join to the posts with mortise-and-tenon joints. The headboard floats in a very wide mortise, pinned only in the center with a screw. The side rails attach to the headboard and footboard posts with bed bolts, which run right through the middle of the mortise-and-tenon, joining the headboard or footboard rail to the post. It makes an excellent bed for a child, but can be made to any size.

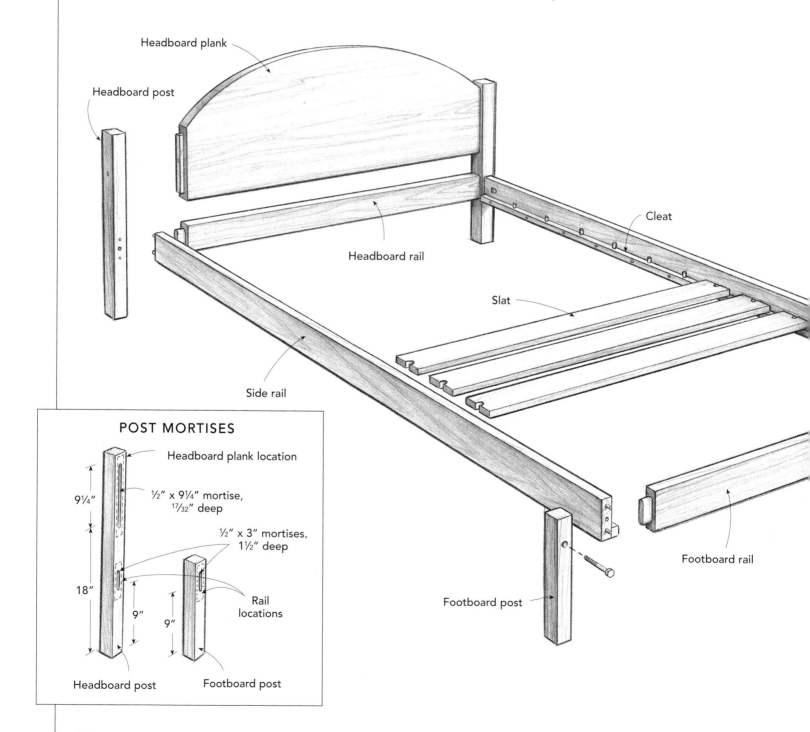

Headboard plank

Headboard post

Headboard rail

Cleat

Slat

Side rail

Footboard rail

Footboard post

POST MORTISES

Headboard plank location

9¼"

½" x 9¼" mortise, ¹⁷⁄₃₂" deep

½" x 3" mortises, 1½" deep

18"

9"

9"

Rail locations

Headboard post

Footboard post

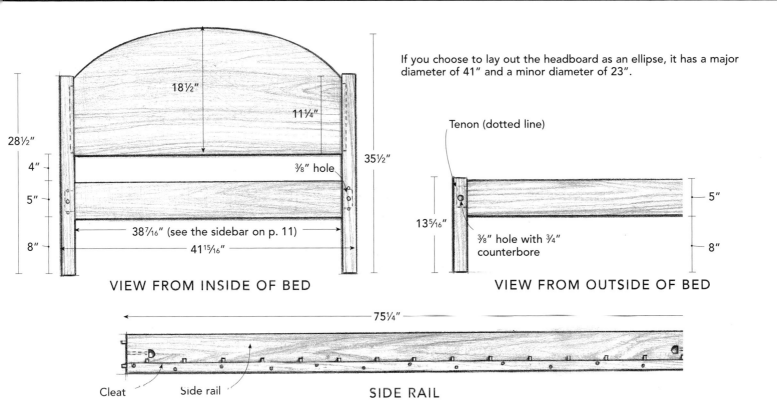

If you choose to lay out the headboard as an ellipse, it has a major diameter of 41" and a minor diameter of 23".

18½"

11¼"

28½"

4"

5"

8"

⅜" hole

38⁷⁄₁₆" (see the sidebar on p. 11)

41¹⁵⁄₁₆"

35½"

VIEW FROM INSIDE OF BED

Tenon (dotted line)

13⁵⁄₁₆"

⅜" hole with ¾" counterbore

5"

8"

VIEW FROM OUTSIDE OF BED

75¼"

Cleat   Side rail

SIDE RAIL

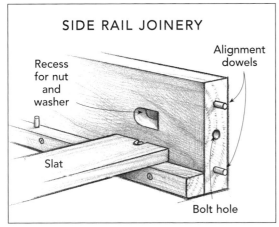

SIDE RAIL JOINERY

Recess for nut and washer

Alignment dowels

Slat

Bolt hole

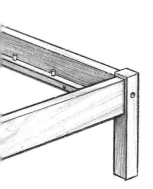

CUT LIST FOR FIRST BED

Headboard and Footboard

2	Headboard posts	1¾ in. x 1¾ in. x 28½ in.
2	Footboard posts	1¾ in. x 1¾ in. x 13⁵⁄₁₆ in.
2	Headboard and footboard rails	1¹⁄₁₆ in. x 5 in. x 41⅜ in.
1	Headboard plank	1¹⁄₁₆ in. x 18½ in. x 39⁷⁄₁₆ in.

Side Rails

2	Side rails	1¹⁄₁₆ in. x 5 in. x 75¼ in.
2	Cleats	1 in. x 1¼ in. x 75⅛ in.
15	Slats	¾ in. x 4 in. x 39 in.

Hardware

4	Hex-head bolts with nuts & washers	⁵⁄₁₆ in. x 5½ in.
8	Dowels (for alignment pins)	⁵⁄₁₆ in. x 1¼ in.
30	Dowels (for slat pins)	⁵⁄₁₆ in. x 1¼ in.
2	#6 x 2½-in. screws	
	#6 x 1¼-in. drywall screws, as needed	

Note: These dimensions are for a twin-size bed. You may have to adjust your dimensions to suit the bed size, the mattress size, or any differences in wood dimensions.

BUILDING THE BED STEP-BY-STEP

THE FIRST BED breaks down into four basic components: the headboard, the footboard, the side rails, and the mattress support. It's best to work on the headboard and footboard at the same time since the work is so similar and you will save set-up time on each of the necessary steps. The side rails come next, since they complete the bed frame. Finally, work on the slats.

HEADBOARD AND FOOTBOARD

Making and mortising the posts

1. Mill the stock for the four posts to 1¾ in. square, then cut them to the lengths indicated in the drawings.

2. Lay out and cut the headboard and footboard rail mortises on the inner faces of the posts. A 3-in.-long, ½-in.-wide, and 1½-in.-deep mortise centered on the width of the post works well for all bed sizes. On a child's bed, locate the bottoms of the mortises 9 in.

up from the bottoms of the posts. On an adult-size bed, the mortises should start 11 in. up from the post bottoms. I use a router and a mortising jig to do this work (see "Mortising Jig for Routing Thin Workpieces").

3. Mark out and cut an additional mortise on each of the headboard posts for the headboard itself. This is a long, shallow mortise—9 in. long, ½ in. wide, and $^{17}/_{32}$ in. deep.

Milling the rails

1. Mill the headboard and footboard rails to size, but not to length. You should also mill the side rails now, since they are the same thickness and width (but then set them aside until you're done with the headboard and footboard).

2. Verify that the thickness of the posts is actually 1¾ in. and that the thickness of the side rails is actually 1¹⁄₁₆ in. before cutting the rails to the indicated length. If you've got parts that are different either by design or by happenstance, you need to calculate the correct rail lengths (see "Determining Rail Lengths" on p. 11).

Tenoning the rails

1. Mark out the location of the tenon so that it's centered on the rail from side to side and from top to bottom. Mark the length of the tenon as well. For both of these tasks, I prefer

> *Tip: If you cut a tenon too loose, you can glue a thin patch of wood onto the cheek. Then re-fit the tenon properly.*

DIMENSIONS FOR OTHER SIZE BEDS

To build this bed in queen or any other size, simply use the dimensions provided below.

Note: Remember to adjust your Cut List accordingly.

	Length between headboard tenons & footboard rails (A)	Width of headboard plank (B)	Overall headboard height (C)	Side rail length
Full	53⅜₆"	19½"	38½"	75¼"
Queen	59⅜₆"	20½"	39½"	80¼"
King	75⅜₆"	22½"	41½"	80¼"
California king	71⅜₆"	22"	41"	86¼"

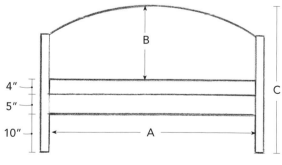

Mortising Jig for Routing Thin Workpieces

This mortising jig holds thin workpieces, such as bed posts, that would otherwise be difficult to mortise with a router. The block is essentially a large piece of wood milled flat and square that supports the router base during the cut. A guide strip keeps the router fence tight to the block during the cut.

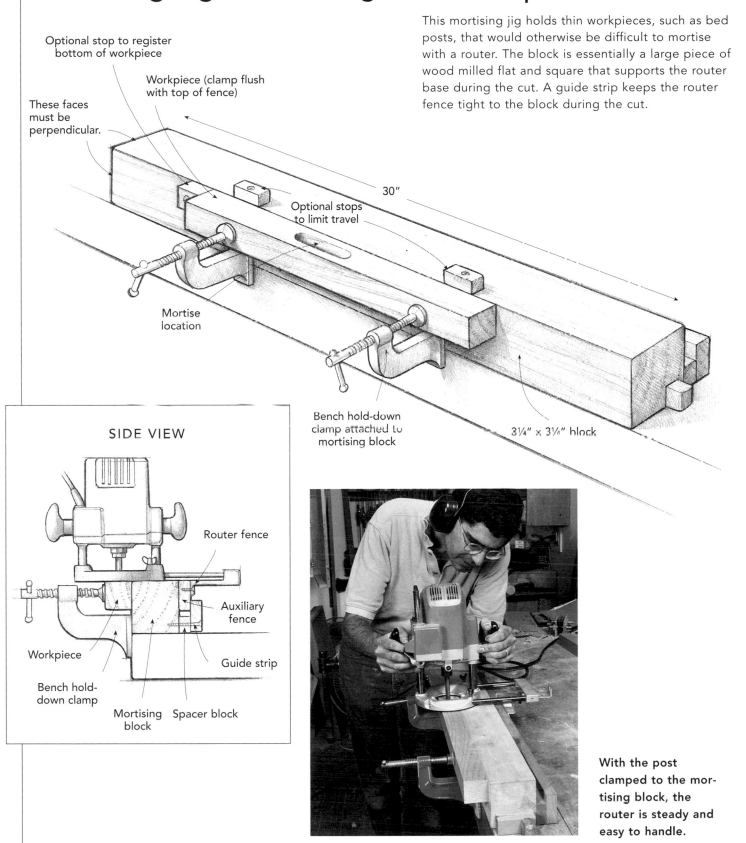

Optional stop to register bottom of workpiece

Workpiece (clamp flush with top of fence)

These faces must be perpendicular.

30"

Optional stops to limit travel

Mortise location

Bench hold-down clamp attached to mortising block

3¼" x 3¼" block

SIDE VIEW

Router fence

Auxiliary fence

Guide strip

Workpiece

Bench hold-down clamp

Mortising block

Spacer block

With the post clamped to the mortising block, the router is steady and easy to handle.

A Tenoning Jig

This jig helps you cut a range of tenons accurately. Its two basic components are a workpiece support, which attaches to the part to be tenoned, and a template, which guides the cuts.

The opening is 6¼" x 3 ½".

FRONT VIEW OF WORKPIECE SUPPORT

Tenoning template

7"

14"

¾"

Runner

9"

12"

3½"

2"

Brace

Fence

Spacer block

22"

6½"

BOTTOM VIEW OF TENONING TEMPLATE

⅜" maple strip

Runner

2⅞"

6¼"

BUILDING THE JIG

1. Assemble all the parts of the main body of the jig (horizontal platform, workpiece support, spacer block, fence, and braces).
2. To align the tenoning template on the horizontal platform so that the guide strip on the template will cut tenons parallel to the edge of the workpiece support, clamp a ¾" thick by 5" wide reference board to the workpiece support so that it extends through the opening in the horizontal platform.
3. Place the tenoning template so the guide strip is lined up exactly with the reference board and clamp the template to the horizontal platform.
4. Screw the two runners to the bottom of the template so they fit tightly against the horizontal platform.

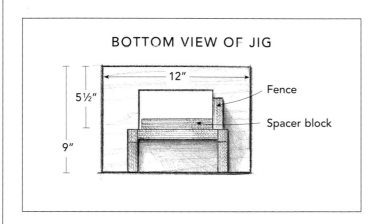

BOTTOM VIEW OF JIG

12"

5½"

9"

Fence

Spacer block

to use a marking gauge, but you can also measure and mark with either a pencil or a knife.

2. Cut away the waste. The tool I use most often to do this job is my plunge router and a special tenoning jig (see "A Tenoning Jig"). The jig works with a plunge router and guide bushing that follows a guide strip to cut the tenon. The location of the tenon can be controlled by where you position the tenoning template on top of the horizontal platform of the workpiece support.

3. Clamp the workpiece to the workpiece support with an edge against the fence and the top flush with the bottom of the tenoning template.

4. Locate the template above the workpiece where you want to cut the tenon, and clamp or screw it in place.

5. Put the router on the jig, and set the plunge mechanism to the right depth. Turn on the router and plunge to the full depth of cut (see "Cross Section of Tenoning Jig in Use" and **photo A**).

6. Cut the tenon waste with many light passes. To cut the other face of the tenon, move over to the opening on the other side of the guide strip.

7. Chisel or cut the waste from the sides of the tenons and round them over with a rasp to match the rounded ends of the mortise (see **photo B** on p. 26).

Tip: When routing the tenons, start with a very shallow climb cut, then waste away the rest of the wood.

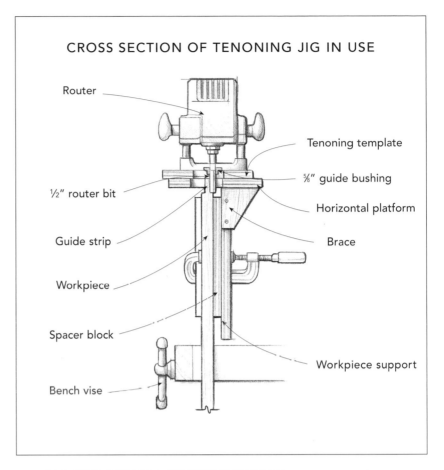

CROSS SECTION OF TENONING JIG IN USE

Router

½" router bit

Guide strip

Workpiece

Spacer block

Bench vise

Tenoning template

⅝" guide bushing

Horizontal platform

Brace

Workpiece support

Photo A: The tenoning jig positions the workpiece upright and supports the router on the end of the rail.

Photo B: Rasping the edges of a tenon is quick and easy. It's a lot easier to make the tenon fit a routed mortise than to square up the ends of the mortise.

8. After you cut the tenons, check the fit of each individually. I use a special rabbet plane to fit the cheeks, but a rasp or sandpaper on a block works also. Be careful not to round over or taper the cheeks. You should have a snug fit that you can put together by hand.

9. Mark the tenon and the corresponding mortise with the same letter or number as soon as you're done fitting them. This will not only remind you where the joint goes, but it also serves as a reminder that you have already fit the joint.

Making the headboard

If you can find a single 18½-in.-wide plank for the headboard, use it. On a table, this would normally lead to warping, but here the long mortises in the posts keep the plank straight. If you do have to glue up the headboard, choose your wood carefully for a good match. Remember, the headboard is usually the visual focus of the bed.

1. Glue up the plank for the headboard (if necessary), let it dry, then make it flat and smooth. Make sure the bottom edge is straight.

2. Figure the length by carefully measuring the shoulder-to-shoulder length of the headboard rail, and add 1 in. for the two ½-in. tenons. Use the rail itself as the ruler to mark off the length.

3. Crosscut the board to length, referencing both cuts off the same edge. You may want to "sneak up" on the proper length, first cutting a little long, then taking a little bit off at a time until the headboard is precisely the right length and exactly square.

4. The headboard should have a nice, gentle curve along the top edge. Mark it by springing a thin piece of wood into a curve using a clamp until you are satisfied with the shape and trace the line with a pencil. Don't cut to the line just yet (see **photo C**).

5. Tenon the ends of the headboard. This is not a normal tenon—it's very wide and very short. The simplest way to do it is to rout both sides of each end with a ½-in. rabbeting bit. Set the depth of cut on the router so you'll leave just over ½ in.—this should mean cutting just under ⁹⁄₃₂ in. deep on both sides of the 1¹⁄₁₆-in.-thick headboard. Back up the headboard where the router exits the cut.

6. Cut the curve on top of the headboard. You can use a bandsaw or a jigsaw, then plane or sand smooth.

7. Mark the headboard tenons 1½ in. from both the bottom and top edges, and cut away the waste. This should leave a tenon that is about 1 in. shorter than the mortise, leaving room for expansion. You don't need to round over the ends of the tenons or square up the ends of the mortises (see **photo D** on p. 29).

8. Fit the tenons to the mortises, and mark both halves of the joint so you'll know what goes where later.

Drilling holes in the posts for the bed bolts

The knockdown joints for the side rails are a simple version of traditional bed bolts. There are three holes to drill in the headboard and footboard posts for each joint—a central bolt hole and two holes for alignment pins made from dowels. The pins align the rail properly and keep it from twisting or shifting.

1. Lay out the locations for the bolt hole in each post. They should be exactly centered on the post and 10½ in. up from the bottom for a child's bed or 12½ in. up from the bottom for a standard twin bed.

2. Lay out the ⁵⁄₁₆-in. holes for the alignment pins 1 in. above and 1 in. below the bolt holes, as measured on centers.

3. To drill the three holes in the posts, I make and use a special jig (see "A Bolt Hole Drilling Guide" on p. 28). The three holes have to align exactly on both the posts and the rails, so consistency is essential. Once you've drilled the ³⁄₈-in. bolt hole in a post (either on the drill press or with a doweling jig), you can use this jig to align the ⁵⁄₁₆-in. holes above and below.

4. The last hole to drill is the counterbored ³⁄₄-in. diameter hole on the outside of the post. If you don't have a ³⁄₄-in. counterboring bit with a ³⁄₈-in. pilot, you should cut this hole before the three on the other side. Mark and drill the ³⁄₄-in. hole about ³⁄₈ in. deep from the outside. Then drill through the center of the hole with a ³⁄₈-in. bit. Then make and use the drilling guide to drill the ⁵⁄₁₆-in. holes from the inside as described above.

Assembling the headboard and footboard

1. Before assembly, carefully plane, scrape, and sand (in whatever combination you prefer) all parts smooth. You might also want to add a small chamfer on all of the edges— about ¹⁄₁₆ in. seems about right. I put a bigger chamfer on the tops of the posts— more like ¹⁄₈ in.—because I think it looks better. On the post bottoms, the chamfer helps keep wood from splitting or chipping off when the bed is moved around.

2. Glue up the headboard first. Spread glue in one of the rail mortises and then very lightly on the corresponding rail tenon. Too much glue on the tenon will lead to squeeze-out. Insert the rail tenon as far as you can by hand, then insert the headboard tenon into the long mortise in the post; however, don't apply any glue to the headboard-post joint. Apply glue to the rail mortise and tenon on the other side.

Photo C: Springing an evenly thin piece of wood into a gentle curve is an easy way to lay out the top of the headboard. You can loosen or tighten the clamp to fine-tune the shape.

A Bolt Hole Drilling Guide

This simple drilling guide ensures consistent placement of the central bolt hole and alignment dowel holes. Use a drill press to make sure the holes are straight. This jig can be used to drill the holes in both the posts and the ends of the side rails.

Hard maple with grain running lengthwise

5"

2½"   2½"   1"

1"

Holes are centered on block

5/16"   3/8"   5/16"

5"

1½"

1½"

⅜" diameter dowel

1 1/16"

WITH GUIDE BUSHINGS

Drill bushing

5/16" hole

For a more durable jig, insert hardened drill bushings for a 5/16-in. drill. Guide should be a little thicker than the bushings are long.

WITH GUIDE STRIP

Drilling guide

Clamp

Rail

Guide strip aligns the jig when used to drill the holes on the rail ends.

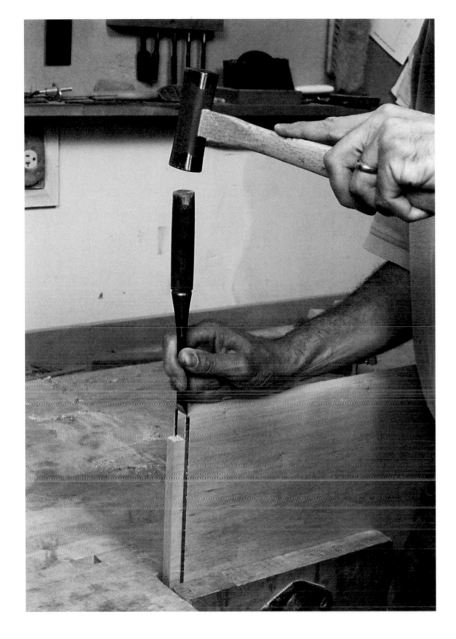

Tip: Yellow glue sets quickly, so you have to move fast. To help with large projects, get everything ready before starting. Check that you have enough clamps and enough room to work. I lay everything out in a way that helps me remember how it all goes together.

Photo D: Chisel away the thin waste left after bandsawing the tenon ends. It's easy to get a precise surface by hand because the chisel is guided by the tenon shoulders.

3. Clamp the assembly together slowly, with one clamp on the front of the assembly and one on the back to equalize the clamping pressure (see **photo E** on p. 30). You may have to adjust the position of the headboard so it's parallel to the rail in order to clamp it up tight.

4. When the headboard is assembled, pin the center in place with a #6 by 2½-in. screw. This also helps keep the shoulder of the headboard tight against the post. Drill the pilot holes so they come through the legs centered on the ends of the headboard. Countersink

the holes about ¼ in. deep so you can plug them after assembly.

SIDE RAILS

Milling and cutting the rails to length

Mill the side rails now if you haven't already, and cut them to length. With a bed made specifically for a child, it's best to leave very little room around the mattress and/or boxspring so the child can't slide down into a

Photo E: When clamping up the headboard assembly, use two clamps on the rail—one in front of the headboard and one behind—and offset them slightly.

gap or shift things around when using the bed as a trampoline—75¼ in. long is fine on this bed. But for an adult bed with just the mattress on a platform of slats, it's better to make the rail between ½ in. and 1 in. longer than the mattress. This leaves room for tucking in the bedding and for taller people to hang their toes off the end.

Drilling holes for the bed bolts

1. Drill the bolt holes for the rail-to-post joints. Because it's not easy to drill perfectly straight holes into the end of a 75-in.-long board, I suggest using a self-centering doweling jig (see **photo F**). Drill as deeply as possi-

ble with the jig, then deepen the hole guiding the drill by hand.

2. Drill the dowel pin locating holes 1 in. deep, using the same jig you made to drill the holes in the posts (see **photo G**). If you didn't make that jig, the self-centering doweling jig will also work.

3. Glue the ⁵⁄₁₆-in. by 1¹⁄₄-in. dowels in the pin holes in the ends of rails.

Routing the nut recesses

1. To cut the recesses for the bed bolt nut on the inside face of each rail, make up a template that will both locate the recess on the rail and create the D shape (see "A Template for Routing Nut Recesses" on p. 32), and clamp it to the inside face.

2. With a ⅜-in. straight bit and a ⅝-in. guide bushing in a plunge router, plunge-cut to a depth no closer than ⅛ in. from the opposite side of the rail, taking very shallow passes. Stop and blow out the sawdust as often as necessary to prevent sawdust from building up in the recess.

3. Chamfer or ease the edges of the recess.

Making and installing the cleats

1. Mill up stock for the two cleats (use scrap from making the side rails if you have it).

2. In one of the 1-in.-wide sides of each cleat, lay out the locations for ⁵⁄₁₆-in. dowel pins. Space them every 5 in., starting 2⁹⁄₁₆ in. from each end (or farther if the cleats are longer).

3. Drill the ⁵⁄₁₆-in.-diameter holes centered on the thickness of the cleat, and make them about ¾ in. deep.

4. Drill a series of countersunk pilot holes for screws in each cleat, every 6 in. or so and in a zigzag pattern about ⅜ in. from each edge—the cleats will be more secure this way. Spread a little glue into each of the dowel holes, and pound in ⁵⁄₁₆-in.- by 1¼-in.-long dowels.

5. Wait until after you apply a finish to the side rails before attaching the cleats. This makes the finishing much easier.

FINAL ASSEMBLY

Making the slats

1. Mill enough wood for 15 slats that are ¾ in. thick, and rip to 4 in. wide.

2. Ease all four edges of each slat by routing with a ¼-in. roundover bit (although anything that breaks the sharp edges is fine).

3. Cut the slats a little bit over finished length for now. To get the exact length, you have to actually set up the bed.

4. Once you've cut each of the slats to length, you can cut the dowel notches in the ends. I do this with a jig (see "A Jig for Notching Bed Slats" on p. 34). However, this jig only works if you're making a small bed or have a fairly high ceiling. If you don't, there is no reason

Photo F: Drill the ⅜-in. bolt hole in the side rail with a self-centering doweling jig. It centers the hole well and is simple to use.

Photo G: To cut the ⁵⁄₁₆-in.-dowel alignment holes in the side rails, use the same drilling guide you used for the posts.

A Template for Routing Nut Recesses

This simple template makes a quick job of cutting the nut recesses on the inside faces of the side rails.

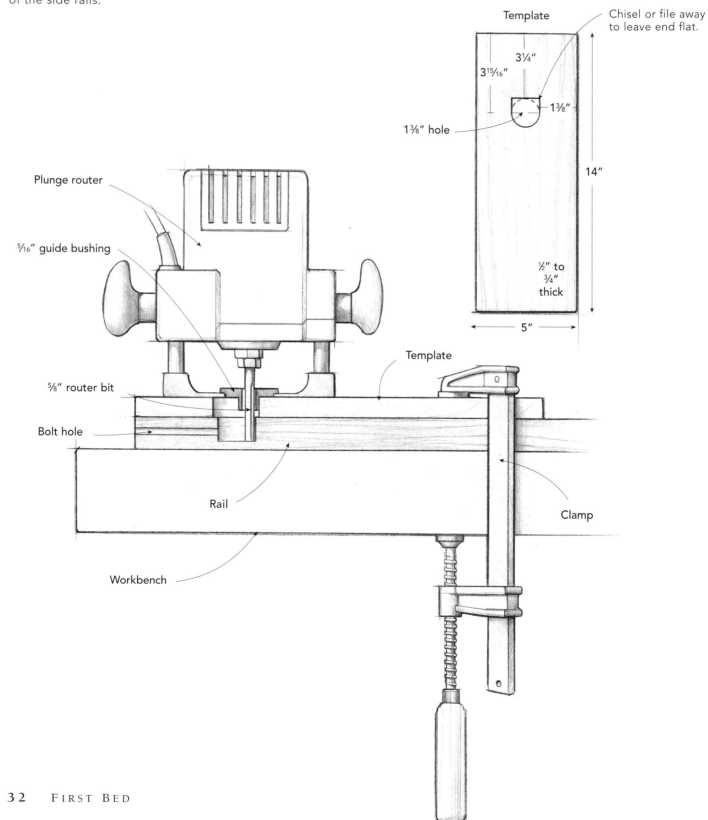

TOP VIEW OF TEMPLATE

Template

Chisel or file away to leave end flat.

$3\frac{1}{4}$"

$3\frac{15}{16}$"

$1\frac{3}{8}$"

$1\frac{3}{8}$" hole

14"

$\frac{1}{2}$" to $\frac{3}{4}$" thick

5"

Plunge router

$\frac{5}{16}$" guide bushing

$\frac{5}{8}$" router bit

Bolt hole

Template

Rail

Clamp

Workbench

you can't cut the notches on the bandsaw and clean them up with a chisel. To check the fit of the slats, you'll have to assemble the bed.

Assembling the parts

1. Attach the cleats once you've finished and waxed the bed (see the Appendix on p. 182 for finishing suggestions). Line them up flush with the bottom of the side rails, and screw in place.

2. To attach the side rails to the headboard and footboard, lean the headboard upright against a wall or something secure, and place the side rails roughly in position. Place a $5/16$-in. by $5\frac{1}{2}$-in. hex-head bolt with a washer and a second washer and nut at each corner.

3. Insert the dowels on one end of a side rail into the corresponding holes in the headboard post. Insert the bolt and washer from the outside of the headboard, until the end of the bolt is just coming into the nut recess. Now place the other washer on the end of the bolt, and thread on the nut. It helps to rotate the bolt from the outside of the bed when you're doing this (see **photo H**).

Tip: Hard maple is the best wood for the slats—it has good stiffness and strength. This is less of a factor with a narrower bed. Any type of wood you can get inexpensively is fine for a twin.

Photo H: To put the bed bolt joints together, insert a bolt with washer from the outside of the bed, until it just reaches into the nut recess. Then place the washer and nut over the end of the bolt, and start turning.

Photo I: To get the second side rail into place, it's easiest to lift the rail in the middle, then work on one end at a time.

A JIG FOR NOTCHING BED SLATS

This jig holds the slats vertically so that perfectly square notches can be cut on the table saw with a dado blade. The jig body is composed of two boards joined at right angles. A fence that straddles the table saw's rip fence guides the jig through the cut.

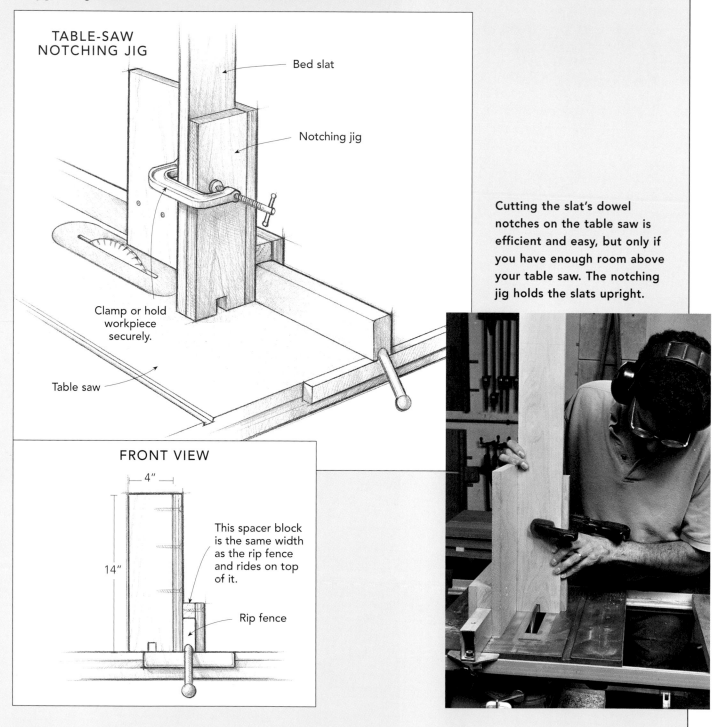

TABLE-SAW
NOTCHING JIG

Bed slat

Notching jig

Clamp or hold
workpiece
securely.

Table saw

FRONT VIEW

4"

14"

This spacer block
is the same width
as the rip fence
and rides on top
of it.

Rip fence

Cutting the slat's dowel
notches on the table saw is
efficient and easy, but only if
you have enough room above
your table saw. The notching
jig holds the slats upright.

Photo J: Drop the slats into place with the notches around the locating pins in the cleats to complete the bed.

4. Use a ½-in. nut driver to tighten up the bolt and a ½-in. open-end wrench to keep the nut from turning. Tighten securely, but don't tighten so hard that you're crushing the wood.
5. Attach the footboard to the other end of the rail the same way you attached the headboard. (Don't try to put the bed together by attaching the second rail before you attach the footboard unless you have help.)
6. Attach the other side rail to the headboard and footboard (see **photo I** on p. 33). Put both of the bolts (with their washers) into the bolt holes in the posts before you pick up the rail. Pushing both bolts into the rail will guarantee that the locating dowels won't accidentally pop out while you work on getting the washers and nuts on. Check to see that all of the bolts are tight.
7. Drop the slats over the dowel pins on the cleats, hoping they fit, and adjusting them if they don't. Then drop the mattress into place (see **photo J**). Voilà. A bed.

SHAKER-STYLE BED

The Shakers lived their lives apart from the "world," what they called life outside their religious communities. They did a lot of things differently from the "world," including sleep. Because the Shakers were celibate, they had little need for double beds and used them only to save space. Two men, women, or children would sleep together in these.

Many Shaker-designed single beds did not break down. The side rails were tenoned into the legs just like the headboards and footboards. Almost all of the beds had casters on the legs. This made it easy to move the bed out of the way when sweeping the floors. The beds were also relatively high off the ground to keep out of the cold drafts near the floor.

This bed is not a copy of a particular Shaker bed. Instead, I have borrowed elements from a number of Shaker beds I have seen. Some of my construction details remain faithful to traditional Shaker construction. But I have made concessions to modern living and to contemporary woodworking techniques.

I chose to make this a full-size bed, which is more useful than the 28-in.- to 34-in.-wide and 70-in.- to 72-in.-long originals. I also omitted the casters. I hesitate to say that these changes make the bed better, but they certainly make it more familiar and comfortable for us today.

Shaker-Style Bed

THE BASIC STRUCTURE of the Shaker-Style Bed is similar to the First Bed. However, the legs are turned, the headboard and footboard planks do double duty as structural rails, and the cleats are integral with the side rail design.

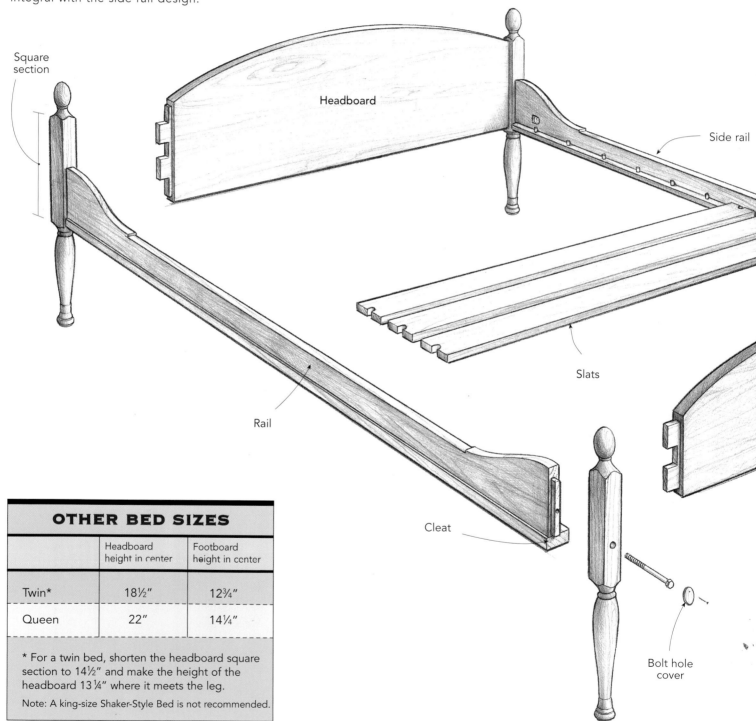

Square section

Headboard

Side rail

Rail

Slats

Cleat

Bolt hole cover

OTHER BED SIZES		
	Headboard height in center	Footboard height in center
Twin*	18½"	12¾"
Queen	22"	14¼"

* For a twin bed, shorten the headboard square section to 14½" and make the height of the headboard 13¼" where it meets the leg.

Note: A king-size Shaker-Style Bed is not recommended.

HEADBOARD DETAILS

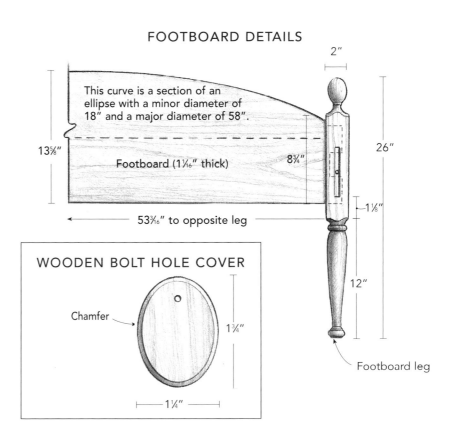

Headboard leg

32"

Shallow mortise

³⁄₈" bolt hole

14¾"

2½"

1⅛"

15⅝"

Headboard (1¹⁄₁₆" thick)

20¾"

53³⁄₁₆" to opposite leg

The overall length of the headboard and footboard planks (including tenons) is 56⅜".

HEADBOARD END OF SIDE RAIL

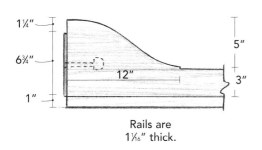

1¼"

6¾"

12"

5"

3"

1"

Rails are 1¹⁄₁₆" thick.

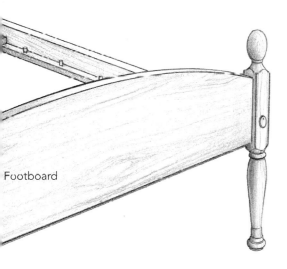

Footboard

FOOTBOARD DETAILS

2"

This curve is a section of an ellipse with a minor diameter of 18" and a major diameter of 58".

13⅝"

Footboard (1¹⁄₁₆" thick)

8¾"

26"

1⅛"

53³⁄₁₆" to opposite leg

12"

Footboard leg

FOOTBOARD END OF SIDE RAIL

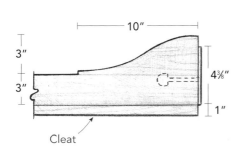

10"

3"

3"

4⅜"

1"

Cleat

WOODEN BOLT HOLE COVER

Chamfer

1¾"

1¼"

BUILDING THE BED STEP-BY-STEP

CUT LIST FOR SHAKER BED

Headboard and Footboard

1	Headboard plank	1¹⁄₁₆ in. x 20¾ in. x 56⅜ in.
1	Footboard plank	1¹⁄₁₆ in. x 13⅝ in. x 56⅜ in.
2	Headboard posts	2 in. x 2 in. x 32¼ in.
2	Footboard posts	2 in. x 2 in. x 26¼ in.

Side Rails

2	Side rails	1¹⁄₁₆ in. x 3 in. x 76½ in.
2	Ogees for headboard ends	1¹⁄₁₆ in. x 5 in. x 12 in.
2	Ogees for footboard ends	1¹⁄₁₆ in. x 3 in. x 10 in.
2	Cleats	1 in. x 2⁵⁄₁₆ in. x 76 in.
15	Slats	¾ in. x 4 in. x 54⅛ in.

Hardware

30	Dowels (for slat pins)	⁵⁄₁₆ in. x 1½ in.
4	Hex-head bolts with nuts and washers	
4	Bolt hole covers	1¼ in. x 1¾ in. x ¼ in. thick
#6 x 1⅝-in. screws, as needed		
#6 x ¾-in. roundhead brass screws, as needed		

These dimensions are for a full-size bed with a mattress up to 8 in. thick. You may have to adjust your dimensions to suit the bed size, the mattress size, or any differences in wood dimensions.

Tip: The moisture in yellow glue swells wood slightly along joint edges. Wait 24 hours before smoothing the surfaces to give the moisture a chance to evaporate and the wood to settle back down.

ALTHOUGH THIS BED looks very different from the First Bed on pp. 18-35, the overall approach to building it is the same. To start, you work on the headboard and footboard together. Then move on to the side rails and finally the mattress support. The turned legs are not essential to the construction, but they are to the design. You can make the bed with straight or tapered legs, but it won't look as nice.

MAKING THE HEADBOARD AND FOOTBOARD

Milling the headboard and footboard planks

1. Mill up the pieces for the headboard and footboard planks.
2. If you're not working with a single board plank, glue the pieces into slightly oversize planks.
3. Cut the planks to size, making sure the edges are parallel and the ends square.

Cutting the tenons

This bed doesn't have a separate headboard and footboard rail to provide structural strength, so the planks themselves need structural tenons. However, 8-in.- to 14-in.-wide mortise-and-tenon joints would break apart due to seasonal wood movement. The traditional solution is to make a divided tenon (see "Headboard and Footboard Joinery" on p. 42).

1. Cut the headboard and footboard plank tenon shoulders with the tenoning jig described in "A Tenoning Jig" on p. 24 and a 4-in.-long straight bit. To use the jig with the wide headboard, remove the vertical fence from the workpiece support. You'll have to cut the tenons a portion at a time (see **photo A**).

Photo A: One good way to cut the full-width tenons on the headboard and foot-board is with the tenoning jig on p. 24 and a 4-in.-long router bit.

2. Lay out the sections of tenon that will stay full length and the short ¼-in. haunches.
3. Cut away the waste on the bandsaw and then pare away all of the haunch tenon on the very top and bottom to leave shoulders.

Laying out and cutting the curve on top of the planks

The headboard and footboard on this bed have elliptical curves. If you're unfamiliar with ellipse layout, see "An Ellipse Layout Jig" on p. 117. You can also use a simple curve as for the First Bed.

1. Lay out either a simple curve or an ellipse along the top edge of the board.
2. Cut the curve out on the bandsaw, keeping to the outside of the line.

3. Clean up the sawn edge with a plane or sandpaper.

Cutting the leg joinery

1. Mill up the leg blanks. The cut list dimensions are ¼ in. longer than finished. The extra ¼ in. on the top of the legs is for the turning centers on the lathe—you'll cut it off and smooth it to shape later.
2. Lay out the mortises for the headboard, footboard, and side rails as shown in "Headboard and Footboard Joinery" on p. 42. Remember that the left and right legs are not identical, though they are symmetrical.
3. Mark lines that indicate the end of the sections that remain square all the way across the

Headboard and Footboard Joinery

Double tenons are the traditional way to join a wide headboard to legs. Wood movement may still cause cracking because the overall movement of the plank is still constrained. But the joints should remain structurally sound. To minimize cracking, make sure the wood is very dry. The haunches are not glued and help keep the headboard from warping.

HEADBOARD LEG BLANK AND TENON

FOOTBOARD LEG BLANK AND TENON

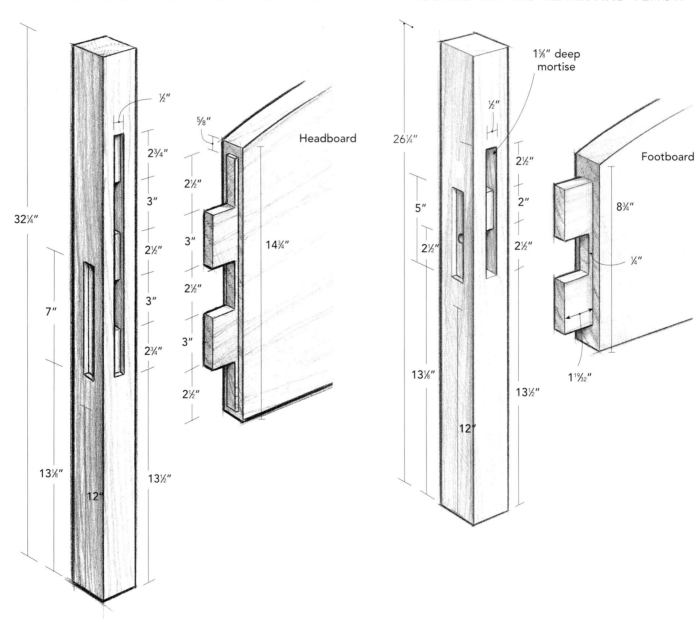

The headboard and footboard planks are structural on this bed. While the traditional construction method is a divided tenon, wood movement may cause cracking because the overall movement of the plank is still constrained. An alternative method is to use a single tenon in the center. This design allows for unconstrained movement and little chance of cracking.

The disadvantage of this technique is that the joint may not keep the headboard plank as tight against the legs. It also offers less glue surface (and strength) than the divided tenons. Using fat haunches (shallow tenons, really) without glue to either side of the tenon helps keep the headboard from warping.

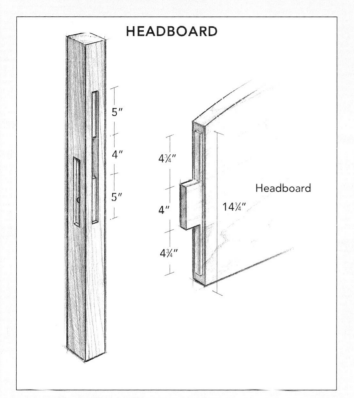

HEADBOARD

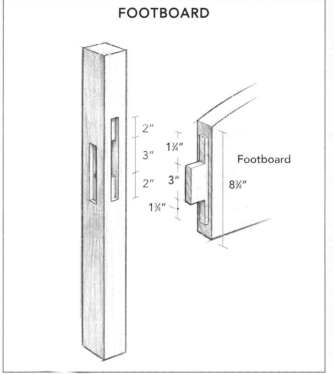

FOOTBOARD

blank at the top and bottom. You need these marks when turning.

4. Cut the side rail mortises ⁹⁄₃₂ in. deep, just deep enough to keep the rail from twisting or moving down. The best tools for the job are a plunge router and the mortising block described in "Mortising Jig for Routing Small Workpieces" on p. 23.

5. Also cut the headboard and footboard mortises ⁹⁄₃₂ in. deep over their full length. Then go back and cut the two full-depth mortises 1⅝ in. deep.

6. Drill the ¾-in.-diameter, ⅜-in.-deep counterbore for the bed bolts on the outside of each leg.

Tip: Use wood with straight, even grain for the legs. You don't want much grain runout on the relatively long and thin legs because it will weaken them considerably.

7. Drill the 5/16-in. holes for the 5½-in. hex-head bed bolts through the legs, centered in the counterbore. To ensure that the bolt hole is straight, drill in from both sides and meet in the middle. It's the long way around to do it, but it ensures a good result.

Turning the legs

1. Make up full-scale patterns of the upper and lower parts of the turnings on pieces of ¼-in. plywood, 2½ in. wide and as long as the section involved (see "Making the Turning Pattern").

2. Set up the blank in the lathe.

3. Set the tool rest in position for roughing out the cylindrical lower leg. Rotate the leg blank by hand to check that the tool rest won't interfere with the blank when it's spinning.

4. Rough out the top and bottom of the blank into cylinders with a roughing gouge, staying about ½ in. away from the edges of the square section.

5. Clean up the transition between cylinder and square section using a gouge, working slowly to the line. Start the cut with the tool up on edge, then roll the gouge flatter toward the bottom of the cut, keeping the bevel rubbing against the spinning leg (see **photo B** on p. 46). If you just present the tool flat (like a scraping tool), you're likely to tear a chunk off the edges of the square section.

6. Using a pencil, transfer the notch locations from the pattern to the spinning blank (see **photo C** on p. 46).

7. Using a parting tool, turn notches in the blank where you have marked it to the various diameters (see "Leg Turning Strategy"). Note that you don't do this on every line you

Making the Turning Pattern

Plywood patterns with notches to hold the tip of a pencil help you mark the turning blank accurately while it's spinning in the lathe.

MAKING THE PATTERN

1. Draw the profiles of the turning on the plywood. Either sketch it out by hand or trace an enlarged photocopy.
2. Draw perpendicular lines out to one edge of the pattern. These will later serve as depth-of-cut and turning-detail guides.
3. At each of these lines, cut a shallow notch with a knife or a saw, just big enough to hold a pencil point.
4. Mark the diameter of the leg at each of the indicated points on the pattern.

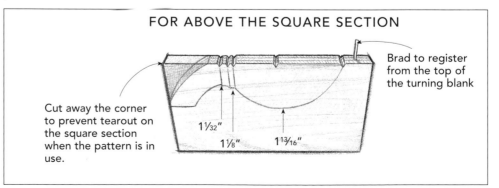

FOR BELOW THE SQUARE SECTION

Brad to register bottom of turning blank

Notches for point of pencil

¼" plywood

1 9/16"
1 1/32"
1¼"   1¼"   1"
1½"
1 7/8"
1 7/8"

FOR ABOVE THE SQUARE SECTION

Cut away the corner to prevent tearout on the square section when the pattern is in use.

Brad to register from the top of the turning blank

1 1/32"
1 1/8"   1 13/16"

marked. Some of the lines indicate the location of a change from one detail to another, and you'll have to turn next to them. On others, such as the sides of the bead below the square section, you can't get a parting tool or calipers into the small space. Size these by eye.

8. Where you can, set your calipers for each desired diameter and reduce the blank with the parting tool until the calipers just fit over the leg at that point (see **photo D** on p. 46).

9. Connect the grooves with the parting tool, following the shape on the pattern. Use whatever turning tools you prefer (see **photo E** on p. 47). Watch the flow of the curves and the overall shape of the leg to make sure you are doing what you want. Correct any problems with a gentle touch.

10. Leave a little pad of wood under the bottom bead for the tailstock to bite into. You can remove the pad later and replace it with a furniture glide, or you can just leave it.

11. Add definition to the turning by touching the sharp tip of a skew chisel to the transition points. Just a touch will do it.

12. Sand the spinning blank with the coarsest grit necessary, working your way up through 400 grit. Be careful not to sand away the crisp

edges of the transition between square section and turning. A good technique is to wrap a 1-in. dowel with sandpaper and work it over the transition while holding on with two hands (see **photo F** on p. 47).

13. Burnish the smooth turning with a handful of clean shavings (see **photo G** on p. 48).

14. Saw off the waste at the very top of the leg above the finial. Then sand to complete the shape.

15. Smooth the faces of the square sections. Because it's important to keep the faces perfectly flat, use a well-tuned handplane. A sanding block that doesn't overhang the edges will also do a good job, though it's more likely to round over the edges.

Assembling the headboard and footboard

1. Fit the headboard joints using a shoulder plane to trim the tenons to size (see **photo H** on p. 48). Strive for a snug fit. The joint should go together with some effort, but heavy hammering should not be necessary.

2. Glue up the headboard and footboard. Spread glue only in the deep mortises; the haunches get no glue at all. You'll need at least two clamps to get the legs tight to the

Tip: The marks you put on the ends of the pommel should be easily visible when the blank is spinning.

LEG TURNING STRATEGY

Use the patterns to reduce the diameter of the turning blank to the desired dimension in a few select places. This will allow you to envision the final leg shape as you turn by "connecting the dots," and help you make duplicates accurately.

Cut the notches with a parting tool.

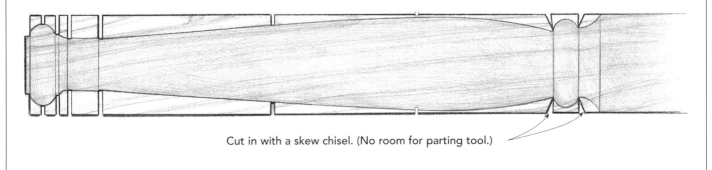

Cut in with a skew chisel. (No room for parting tool.)

Photo B: After roughing out the cylinder below the joinery block, you have to cut the transition from square to round carefully. The gouge should be up on edge as you start the cut at the line.

Photo C: Touching a pencil point lightly in each of the notches on the turning pattern leaves an easily visible mark on the round leg blank. These marks will guide your cuts.

Photo D: Hold the calipers with one hand and the parting tool with the other hand. The calipers will drop over the sized notch when you turn to the correct diameter.

Photo E: After roughing out the shape of this part of the leg with a gouge, finish up the cut with a skew chisel.

tenon shoulders. Check that the tenons are not too long for their mortises. They should be about $\frac{1}{32}$ in. short. Otherwise when you glue up, the joint may not come fully together.

MAKING THE SIDE RAILS AND SLATS

1. Mill up the 3-in.-wide rails, getting a flat and smooth surface on both edges because you'll have glue joints on both.

2. Crosscut to $77\frac{1}{2}$ in. long, which leaves 1 in. of extra length.

3. Smooth the top edge of the rail with a handplane now so you won't have to do this with the blocks attached. You can do this later with a scraper and sandpaper, if you prefer (or if you forget, as I did).

Adding ogee blocks to the side rails

1. Rip the four ogee blocks to width, 5 in. for the headboard blocks and 3 in. for the foot-board blocks. Find boards that match well in color and grain so the joint between the blocks and the rail isn't obvious. Also make sure the end grain of the block matches that of the rail (see "Grain Orientation on the Side Rails" on p. 49).

Photo F: Sand the transition from square to round using a sanding dowel so you don't blur the edges sanding by hand.

Photo G: Burnish the leg with a handful of clean shavings after all the sanding is done.

2. Joint the bottom edge of the stock straight and smooth.

3. Cut the headboard blocks to 12½ in. long and the footboard blocks to 10½ in. long. This leaves ½ in. extra: ¼ in. for waste and ¼ in. for the tenon.

4. Lay out the ogee shape on each block and bandsaw to shape. Smooth the rough edges with spokeshaves, scrapers, and sandpaper.

5. Line up the blocks with the ends of the rails and glue them in place using cauls made from the cutoffs (see **photo I** on p. 50).

6. Cut the rail ends square and to their finished length of 76½ in. after the glue dries.

Cutting the stub tenons

The side rails use a short tenon instead of two dowels to align and reinforce the rail-to-leg joint against twist and shear forces.

Photo H: Trimming the cheeks of the tenons to fit the mortises is easy with a shoulder plane. Note that you cut across the grain.

1. Rout the stub tenon shoulder. Either use the jig shown in "A Tenoning Jig" on p. 24, or just rout rabbets on both sides of each end with the base of the router running on the face of the rail.

2. Cut away some of the tenon to create the top shoulder. Don't do this on the bottom because the added cleat will create the shoulder on that side. Chisel the remainder flush with the shoulder surface.

Drilling for the bed bolts and making recesses for the nuts

1. Locate the bed bolt holes 2½ in. up from the bottom of the rail (not including the cleat). This puts the nut in the full length portion of the rail and not in the ogee blocks.

2. Drill in from the end of the rail for the bolt holes with a ⅜-in. drill bit using a doweling jig for accuracy.

3. If you need to extend the hole deeper than the jig will allow, drill the rest by hand—it will follow the existing hole well.

4. Rout or drill and chisel a recess for the nut, as described in "A Template for Routing Nut Recesses" on p. 32. The only difference is the location for the recess. The flat side of the recess should be 3¼ in. from the shoulder of the rail and centered on the bolt hole.

Making and adding the cleats to the rails

The cleats that support the slats on this bed are screwed to the bottoms of the rails instead of to the sides. Try to use boards that match the color and grain of the rails.

1. Cut cleats exactly to the length of the side rails between the tenons.

2. Plane or sand the outside edge of the cleats smooth.

3. Drill a series of pilot holes for # 6 by 1⅜-in. screws to attach the cleat to the side rail. Drill from the bottom, ⅝ in. from the outside edge of the cleat and every 4 in. If you start 1½ in. from each end, you should wind up with 19 screw holes (see "Cleat Details" on p. 51).

4. Drill the holes on the top face of the cleat for the dowel pins that hold the slats in place. These are ⁵⁄₁₆-in. holes, ¾ in. deep. Locate the holes ⅝ in. from the inside edge of the cleat, spaced every 5 in. starting 2½ in. from each end.

5. Squirt a little glue into each hole, then pound in a ⁵⁄₁₆-in. by 1½-in. dowel.

6. Scribe a line with a marking gauge ¹⁄₁₆ in. from the outside edge of the cleat. This is the reference line along which you glue the rail.

7. Spread a light film of glue on the bottom of the side rail, keeping glue away from the outside edge to minimize the squeeze-out.

8. Place the rail on the cleat along the scribed line and flush with the ends of the cleat. Clamp in place.

Tip: To pare the very top edge of the tenon shoulder flush, tap down with a ¾-in. chisel, flat side against the shoulder. The shoulders of the tenon will keep the chisel aligned.

GRAIN ORIENTATION ON THE SIDE RAILS

Ideally, the grain on the different parts of the side rail should run in the same basic direction.

Boards with mixed grain

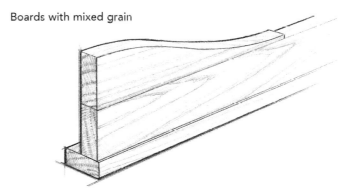

Boards with grain running in same direction

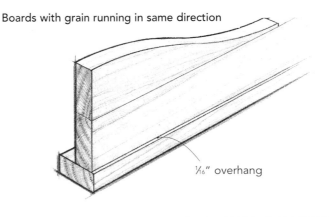

¹⁄₁₆" overhang

Photo I: It's easy to clamp the shaped blocks to the side rails if you use cauls made from cutoffs left over from making the blocks (painted darker for better visibility).

Photo J: Both of these wooden bolt hole covers look good with the bed. Choose for yourself.

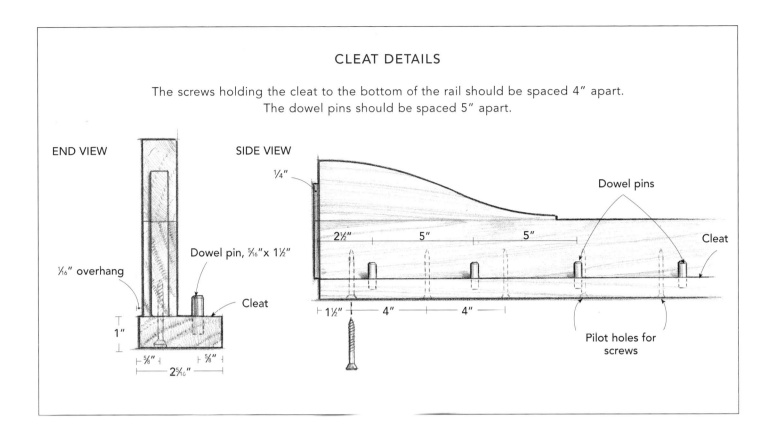

CLEAT DETAILS

The screws holding the cleat to the bottom of the rail should be spaced 4" apart.
The dowel pins should be spaced 5" apart.

END VIEW

SIDE VIEW

$\frac{1}{4}$"

Dowel pins

2½"   5"   5"

Cleat

Dowel pin, $\frac{5}{16}$" x 1½"

$\frac{1}{16}$" overhang

Cleat

1"

1½"   4"   4"

$\frac{5}{8}$" $\frac{5}{8}$"

$2\frac{5}{16}$"

Pilot holes for screws

9. Drive screws into the holes one at a time, checking to be sure the rail and cleat stay properly aligned.

Making the bolt hole covers

You can purchase bolt hole covers for this bed, or you can make your own out of wood. The wood ones are simple to make and are more traditional. You can either make 1³/₁₆-in. by 1¹¹/₁₆-in. rectangles of ¼-in.-thick stock, or cut out ovals (see **photo J**).

1. To make either square or round bolt hole covers, cut them to size, sand the edges smooth, then chamfer the outside face with a plane or sandpaper.
2. Drill ⁹/₆₄-in.-diameter holes in the tops and ¹/₁₆-in. or ⁵/₆₄-in. pilot holes in the legs,

about ⅜ in. above the top of the counterbored bolt hole.
3. Secure the covers with #6 by ¾-in. round-head brass screws.

Making the slats

All that remains is making the bed slats and finishing the bed.

1. Make the ¾-in.-thick, 4-in.-wide bed slats out of maple. To get the exact length, you should assemble the bed first and measure the distance inside the rails.
2. Notch the ends on the bandsaw with a router or upright on the table saw, as described in "A Jig for Notching Bed Slats" on p. 34. Drop each slat into place over the dowel pins, then lift the mattress into place.

Pencil-Post Bed

Beds with four tall posts at the corners have been around since the Middle Ages. In the early history of the bed, the posts held heavy drapes that both created a more private space and helped retain some heat in otherwise poorly heated rooms. The Pencil-Post Bed is one of many variations of this form and lightens it up considerably. What I like so much about this particular type of bed is the distilled simplicity.

This is the only bed in the book that can be built almost entirely without glue. There aren't any glued joints. You may have to glue up the headboard plank out of narrower boards, but once that's done, you can pretty much put the glue bottle away.

On all of the other beds, the headboard and footboard are assemblies. On the Pencil-Post Bed, each of the posts and rails remains separate. All these parts are held together with bolts. Dry tenons hold the headboard in place on the posts, and the bolted connections between the headboard rail and the posts capture the headboard securely in place. Why is this? The bed has to disassemble into single parts or it would be almost impossible to move out of any one room into another. If you glued the headboard up in your shop, you might have to sleep in your shop.

Pencil-Post Bed

AS THERE ISN'T MUCH HIDDEN in this bed, this exploded view is really an unbolted view. Note how the bolts for the headboard and footboard rails are off-set from the side rail bolts. The headboard plank is tenoned into the headboard posts, but the tenons just hold the headboard in position. The bolts holding the posts to the rails keep the headboard securely in place.

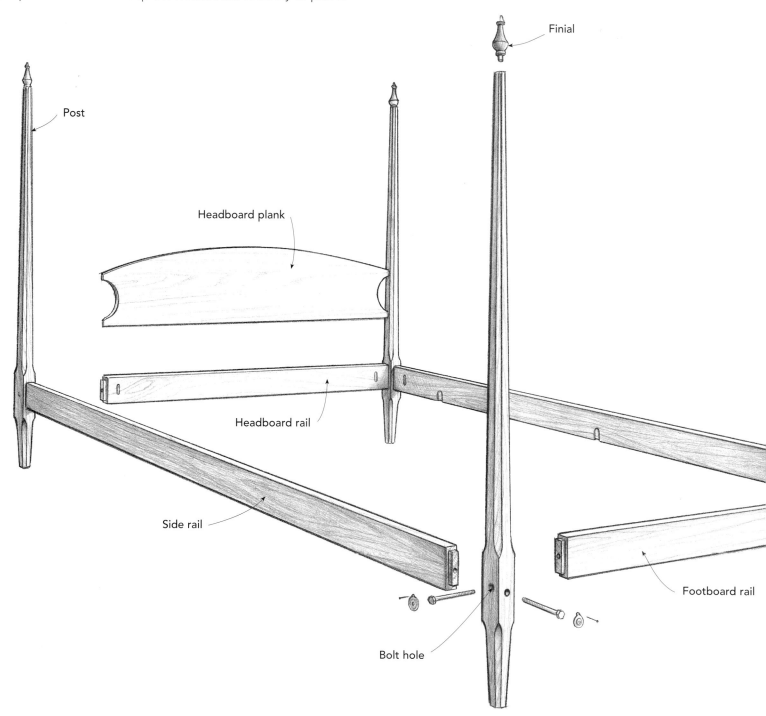

Finial

Post

Headboard plank

Headboard rail

Side rail

Footboard rail

Bolt hole

HEADBOARD

View is from inside bed

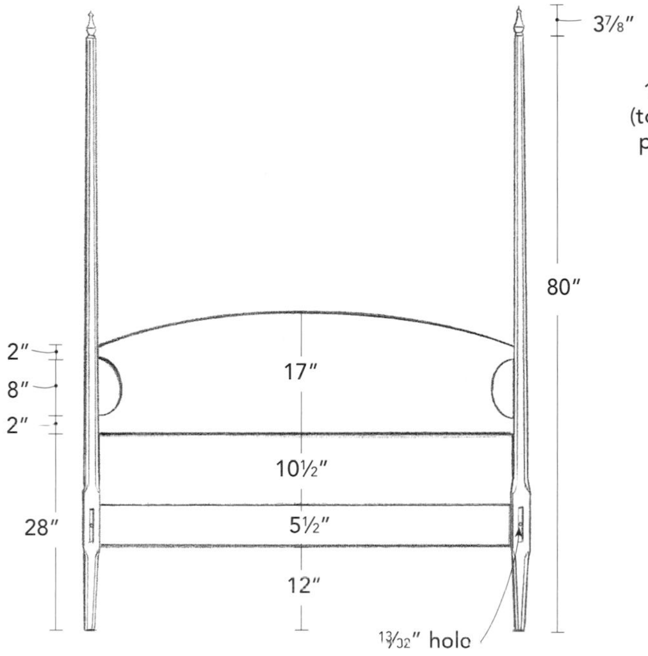

3⅞"
80"
2"
8"
2"
28"
17"
10½"
5½"
12"
13/32" hole

FOOTBOARD

View is from outside bed

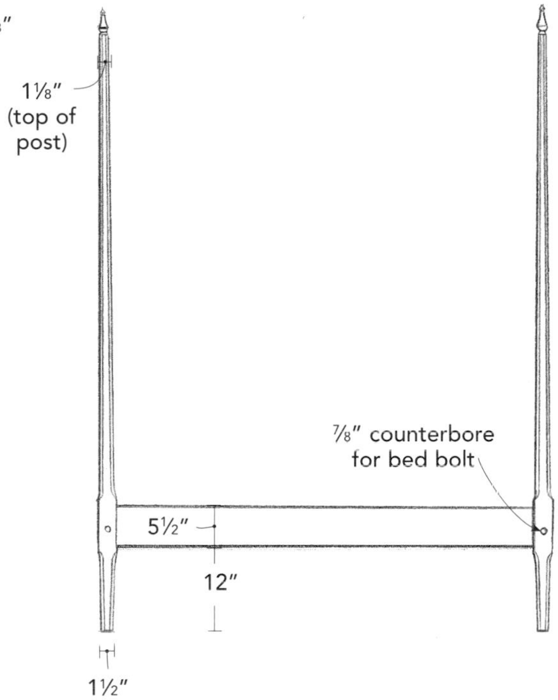

1⅛"
(top of
post)
⅞" counterbore
for bed bolt
5½"
12"
1½"

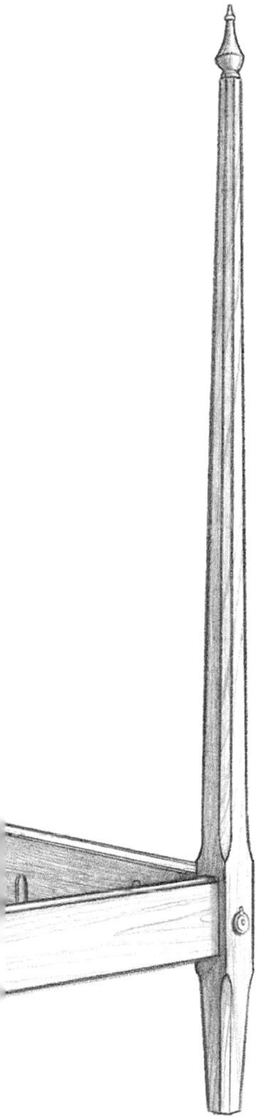

CUT LIST FOR PENCIL-POST BED

Headboard and Footboard		
4	Posts	2¾ in. x 2¾ in. x 80 in.
2	Headboard and footboard rails	1¾ in. x 5½ in. x 60¼ in.
1	Headboard plank	1¼ in. x 17 in. x 61¼ in.
4	Finials (turning blanks)	1¾ in. x 1¾ in. x 4¾ in.
2	Tester rails (head and foot)	⅝ in. x 1 1/16 in. x 63 1/16 in.
2	Tester rails (side)	⅝ in. x 1 1/16 in. x 83 13/16 in.
Side Rails		
2	Side rails	1¾ in. x 5½ in. x 81 in.
Hardware		
8	Traditional bed bolts	
6	Mattress hangers and screws	
4	Dowel pins	⅜ in. x 2 in.
8	Brass bolt hole covers and screws	

These dimensions are for a queen-size bed with a box spring and mattress. You may have to adjust your dimensions to suit the bed size, the mattress size, or any differences in wood dimensions.

BUILDING THE BED STEP-BY-STEP

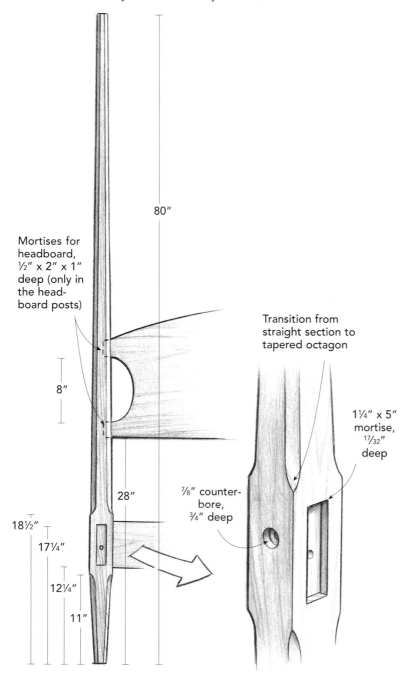

POST DETAILS

The posts are the single most complex part to make. Cut all the joinery in the posts before you taper them, and you'll save many headaches.

80"

Mortises for headboard, ½" x 2" x 1" deep (only in the headboard posts)

8"

Transition from straight section to tapered octagon

1¼" x 5" mortise, 17/32" deep

28"

⅞" counterbore, ¾" deep

18½"

17¼"

12¼"

11"

THE PENCIL-POST BED breaks down into a collection of nine major parts: four posts, four rails, and the headboard. The box spring is supported by cast-iron brackets screwed to the side rails. You can add either finials or a tester to detail the tops of the posts. The work progresses from posts to rails to the headboard since the finished posts are helpful to drill the rails accurately, and the headboard dimensions should come from a test-fit of the headboard posts and rail.

THE POSTS

Milling the posts

As you might expect, most of the work on the Pencil-Post Bed goes into the posts. The basic milling, mortising, and shaping of the posts accounts for almost half of this project. Fortunately, the work is interesting and rewarding.

Mill up stock for four posts, 2¾ in. square and 80 in. long. Try to find 12/4 stock for the posts. If you can't, glue them up from 8/4 stock. Two layers of 6/4 stock do not make 2¾ in. thick once jointed and planed.

Mortising and drilling the posts

1. Look at the posts and decide where you want them on the bed. Mark the intended position of each post on the bottom, close to

Tip: If you glue up boards for the posts, try to put pieces with similar grain together, both in terms of appearance and orientation. Gluing together quartered and flatsawn boards is an invitation to trouble later. And try to keep the seam between the layers centered in the posts.

LAYING OUT TAPERS ON THE POST BLANKS

Tapers give the posts definition and lightness. They're also easy to cut.

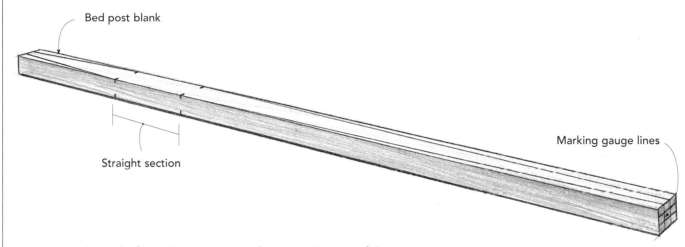

Bed post blank

Marking gauge lines

Straight section

1. Mark out the finished dimensions on the top and bottom of the posts. For the top, set the marking gauge to $1\frac{3}{16}$". For the bottom, set it to $\frac{5}{8}$".
2. Mark the limits of the straight sections with a pencil and a square. They're located from 11" to $18\frac{1}{2}$" up from the bottom of each post.
3. Draw straight lines between the corners of the straight section and the finished dimension marks on the upper and lower sections of each post— but only on one face of each post. If you mark the tapers on adjacent faces before cutting the first two tapers, you'll just cut off the marks for the second face when you bandsaw the first.

the center. This way the marks will survive the shaping process.

2. Lay out the rail mortise locations on all four posts. They are all centered on the posts and located between $12\frac{1}{4}$ in. and $17\frac{1}{4}$ in. up from the bottoms (see "Post Details").

3. Rout the mortises with a plunge router, $\frac{1}{2}$-in. straight bit, and fence. The posts are wide enough to rout without any additional support. Make the cut in two passes, one from each side of the post.

4. Mark out the locations for the bolt holes, staggering them so they do not intersect. Make sure you stagger them consistently, with low ones for the side rails and high ones for the headboard and footboard or vice versa.

5. Drill the $\frac{7}{8}$-in. counterbores for the bolt heads in the outside faces of the posts about $\frac{3}{4}$ in. deep.

6. Drill the $\frac{25}{64}$-in. or $\frac{13}{32}$-in. bolt holes about halfway through the post from the outside.

7. Measure and mark the locations of the holes on the inside faces of the posts (in the mortises), and drill back to meet the bolt holes. Of course, you could also drill before mortising and avoid this trouble. You could also do all of the drilling after you've cut the posts to shape (as you see in the photographs), but only if you forget to do it now (as I did).

Tip: Set up the router to cut on the far side of the post from the fence. This way, if the fence slips from the post when routing, the mistake can be cut away on the next pass.

Post-Tapering Jigs

You can use these jigs either with a bandsaw or with a table saw that has enough blade height to cut through the 3½" combined thickness of the jig and the post.

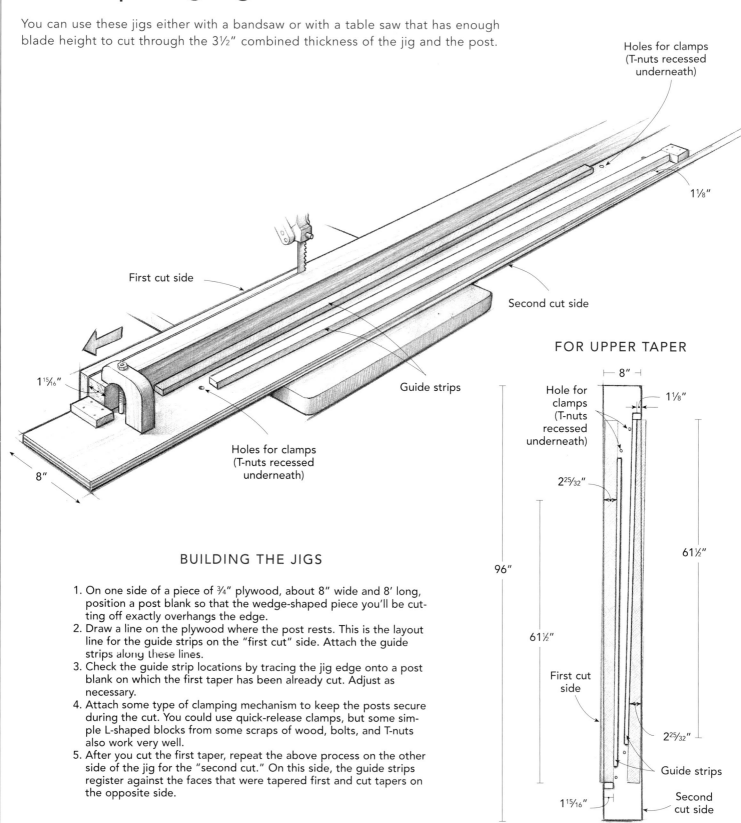

Holes for clamps (T-nuts recessed underneath)

1⅛"

First cut side

Second cut side

Guide strips

1¹⁵⁄₁₆"

8"

Holes for clamps (T-nuts recessed underneath)

FOR UPPER TAPER

8"

Hole for clamps (T-nuts recessed underneath)

1⅛"

2²⁵⁄₃₂"

96"

61½"

61½"

First cut side

2²⁵⁄₃₂"

Guide strips

1¹⁵⁄₁₆"

Second cut side

BUILDING THE JIGS

1. On one side of a piece of ¾" plywood, about 8" wide and 8' long, position a post blank so that the wedge-shaped piece you'll be cutting off exactly overhangs the edge.
2. Draw a line on the plywood where the post rests. This is the layout line for the guide strips on the "first cut" side. Attach the guide strips along these lines.
3. Check the guide strip locations by tracing the jig edge onto a post blank on which the first taper has been already cut. Adjust as necessary.
4. Attach some type of clamping mechanism to keep the posts secure during the cut. You could use quick-release clamps, but some simple L-shaped blocks from some scraps of wood, bolts, and T-nuts also work very well.
5. After you cut the first taper, repeat the above process on the other side of the jig for the "second cut." On this side, the guide strips register against the faces that were tapered first and cut tapers on the opposite side.

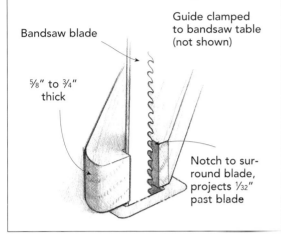

FLUSH-TRIMMING GUIDE FOR THE BANDSAW

The edge of the tapering jig rides against the nose of this guide. It does not interfere with the cutting.

Bandsaw blade

Guide clamped to bandsaw table (not shown)

⅝" to ¾" thick

Notch to surround blade, projects 1/32" past blade

FOR LOWER TAPER

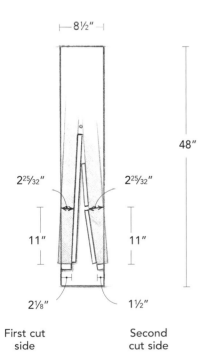

⊢—8½"—⊣

48"

2²⁵/₃₂"   2²⁵/₃₂"

11"   11"

2⅛"   1½"

First cut side   Second cut side

Photo A: The hold-down clamp in the foreground is a block and a bolt threaded into a recessed T-nut on the bottom of the jig.

Cutting the tapers on the posts

There are several good ways to taper the four sides of the posts: cut by eye on the bandsaw or use a jig on the bandsaw or on the table saw. Freehand cutting on the bandsaw is simple but requires pretty good technique for a straight cut over such a long distance. The jig alternatives are more involved, but guarantee results.

1. Mark out the tapers on the posts (see "Laying Out Tapers on the Post Blanks" on p. 57).

2. Make two tapering jigs, one for the upper taper and one for the lower taper (see "Post-Tapering Jigs"). The jigs work equally well on either the bandsaw or the table saw.

3. On the bandsaw, the jigs ride against the flush-trimming guide. Set the trimming guide to cut 1/32 in. shy of the taper layout lines (see **photo A**).

Photo B: On a table saw with a blade that can be raised to at least 3½ in., the tapering jigs work very well. Clamp a piece of plywood on the other side of the blade to prevent the wedge-shaped cutoff from dropping through the throat plate.

Tip: You can taper smaller pieces of wood on the jointer safely but don't try it with 7-ft.-long posts. It's dangerous and you'll never get the angle right.

4. On the table saw, set the rip fence to $\frac{1}{32}$ in. wider than the plywood tapering jig. The opposite edge of the jig rides against the rip fence as the sawblade cuts the post almost flush with the jig (see **photo B**).

5. Cut the tapers to the outside of the lines on either the bandsaw or the table saw, leaving enough room to clean up the cuts. With both jigs, you cut tapers on two adjacent faces with the post on the "first cut" side of the jig, then switch over to the "second cut" side for the remaining two faces.

6. Save the cutoffs from the tapering of the upper part of the post—you'll need them when cutting the mortises for the headboard plank.

7. Clean up the tapered faces with a hand-plane or by sanding. Try to avoid cutting into the straight section.

Giving the posts eight sides

When tapered, the posts are only half done. The tapers still need to be cut into an octagonal profile.

1. Lay out the edges of four new facets along the tapered portions of the posts (see "Two Octagon Layout Methods."

2. If you use the layout jig, practice with it a few times on some scraps of ¾-in. wood. It's not the easiest jig to use because the points tend to wander.

3. When confident, clamp the post securely so you can use two hands on the jig, and scribe the octagon lines.

Two Octagon Layout Methods

You can lay out the octagon one of two ways. The first is by determining the octagon profile and drawing the lines with a straightedge. The second entails building a simple jig.

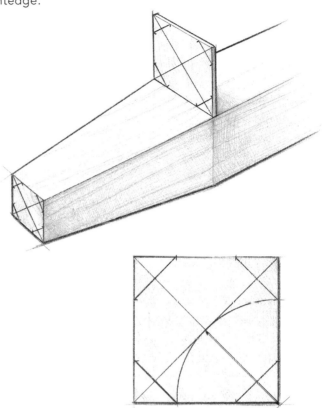

DRAWING AN OCTAGON PROFILE

The distance from a corner to the center of the square, when transferred to the sides of the square, defines the corners of the octagon.

1. Draw three different-size squares: one that's the same dimensions as the very top of the post, one of the bottom, and one the size of the straight section (2¾" by 2¾") that you will use at the top and bottom of this section.
2. Draw the two diagonals to find the center of each square.
3. Set a compass to the distance from one of the corners to the center of the square.
4. With the compass point in the corner of the square, mark the sides of the square. Repeat this process from the other corners, and you'll locate the points where the octagon sides meet.
5. Transfer the dimensions from the drawn octagons to the faces of the posts.
6. Connect the points on the post with a straightedge to create the edges of the octagonal facets.

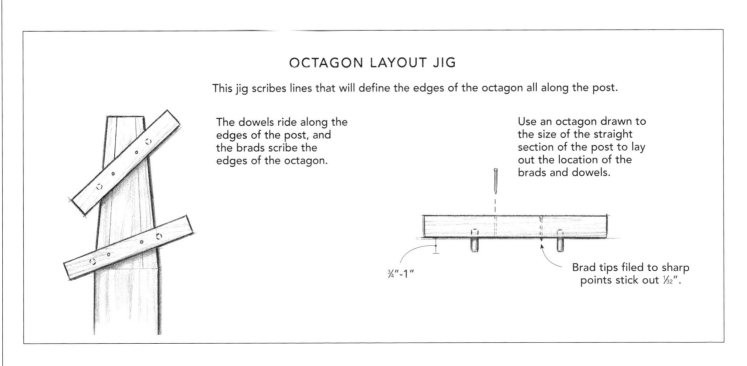

OCTAGON LAYOUT JIG

This jig scribes lines that will define the edges of the octagon all along the post.

The dowels ride along the edges of the post, and the brads scribe the edges of the octagon.

Use an octagon drawn to the size of the straight section of the post to lay out the location of the brads and dowels.

¾"-1"

Brad tips filed to sharp points stick out 1⁄32".

A Jig for Cutting Tapered Octagons

This jig supports the post when bandsawing the angled facets to make an octagon.

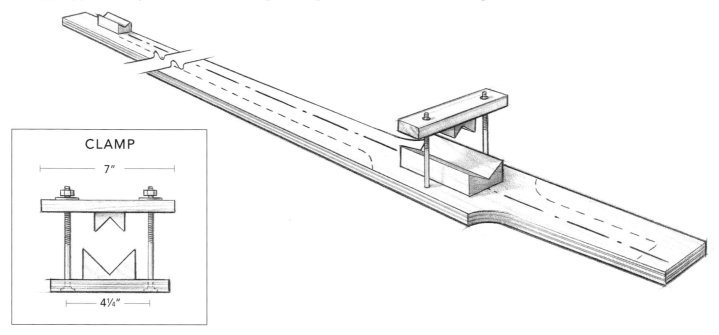

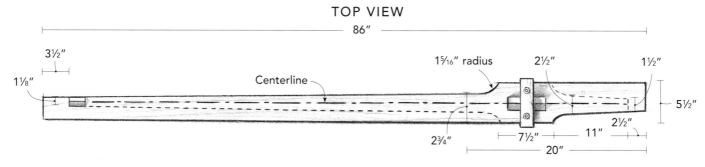

CLAMP

7"

4¼"

TOP VIEW

86"

3½"

1⅛"

Centerline

1⁵⁄₁₆" radius

2½"

1½"

5½"

2¾"

2½"

7½"

11"

20"

Start to cut the octagon sides at the ends of the posts. Starting at the square sections will cause problems.

MAKING AND USING THE JIG

1. Lay out the profile of a post (with a fat straight section) in the center of a piece of ¾" plywood that's 5½" wide and 86" long. Draw in a centerline.
2. Cut away and smooth the jig to the profile line of the post as shown in the drawing. You'll want to make your jig the mirror image of mine if you bandsaw's throat is on the left side (open on the right).
3. Make and attach a clamp at the bottom and a support near the front to hold the post securely.
4. Use the jig with the same flush-trimming guide you used for the four-sided taper jig.
5. The jig works better when you cut in from an end than when you try to cut from the straight section. That's why you cut only one side of the upper and lower profiles on the jig.
6. Rotate the post and cut the next facets. Repeat until the octagons are complete.

4. Make a jig to support the post for cutting the facets on the bandsaw and cut the facets (see "A Jig for Cutting Tapered Octagons"). You can also cut the octagonal profile by hand (see "Cutting the Octagonal Profile by Hand").
5. Clean up the four new facets with a well-tuned handplane. Sight from the ends of the post frequently to see if you're planing straight. Once you're close to the finished depth along the whole length, take fine cuts with the plane. Try for full-length passes at the very last.

Shaping the transition from octagonal facet to straight section

The transition from straight section to octagon takes the form of a curve about ¾ in. long (see "Post Details" on p. 56).

1. Make a cardboard pattern of the desired curve and then mark each of the facet faces. This way, you can cut to the lines on the curves as well as on the straight tapers.
2. Use a curved-sole spokeshave or a rasp with a rounded face to rough out the transition.
3. Scrape and sand with sandpaper wrapped around a 1½-in.-diameter dowel to smooth the transitions (see **photo C** on p. 64).
4. Finally, plane or sand a small (1/32 in. or less) chamfer around the top and bottom edges of each post.

Mortising for the headboard

1. Place a post on the bench, with the facet to be mortised face up. Take a pair of cutoffs from the initial tapering of the posts and clamp them on either side of the location where you will cut the mortises, with wide ends toward the top. The wedges basically extend the straight section of the post, and if clamped flush with the top facet, they'll also support the router more fully.
2. If you didn't save the cutoffs, make up some wedges with an angle the same as the taper.
3. Mark out the locations for the mortises (see "Post Details" on p. 56), and plunge-cut

CUTTING THE OCTAGONAL PROFILE BY HAND

Cutting the octagonal taper by hand is not a bad option. There are no special tools required, and it doesn't take all that long (10 minutes to 15 minutes per facet). However, figured grain can be *really* difficult to cut smoothly.

1. Set up the post in some notched blocks on your workbench to hold it at a 45-degree angle.
2. To remove wood in a hurry, start with a drawknife or plane set for a *deep* cut.
3. Switch to a plane set for a light cut as you get closer to the layout lines. Keep your eyes on both layout lines to cut at the right angle.
4. Skew your plane to get closer to the transition blocks. Switch to a spokeshave to cut right up to the transition from taper to straight section.

Skew the plane to one side so you can start the cut down the post as close as possible to the straight sections.

Photo C: It takes a twisting motion with the sandpaper-wrapped dowel to clean up the curved transition area between the square joinery block and the octagonal post effectively.

with a router 1 in. deep (see **photo D**). You can also drill out the waste wood and chop the mortises by hand.

4. Chisel the ends of the mortises square and chamfer the mortise edges very lightly.

MAKING THE RAILS

Milling the rail stock

1. Mill rail stock for the side, headboard, and footboard rails, and cut them to length (see "Rail Details").

2. Cut the tenons on the ends of the rails on the table saw with a dado blade or with a router using a 1/2-in. rabbeting bit. To support the router when cutting the narrow sides, clamp a pair of rails together (see **photo E**).

3. Rout the wider faces to complete the tenons (see **photo F**).

Drilling for the bolts

The easiest way to drill the bed bolt holes in the ends of the rails is to use the holes in the posts as a drilling guide.

1. Clamp a headboard or footboard rail upright in a bench vise, and hold the appropriate post in place. Make sure you've matched up the correct post with the rail

Photo D: The author clamped the wedge-shaped cutoffs from the tapering operation (darkened for better visibility in the photograph) on either side of the post to provide a straight reference edge for routing the headboard mortises.

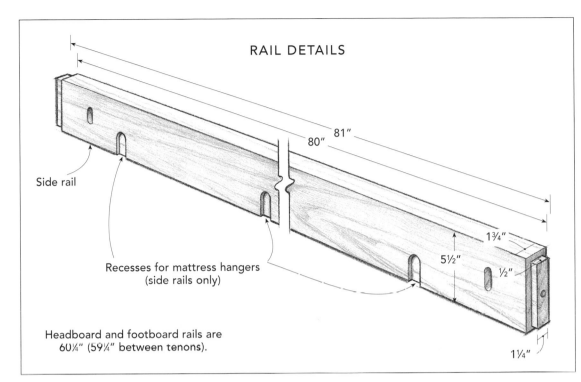

RAIL DETAILS

81"

80"

Side rail

Recesses for mattress hangers
(side rails only)

Headboard and footboard rails are
60¼" (59¼" between tenons).

1¾"

5½"

½"

1¼"

Tip: *When routing
tenons using a
rabbeting bit, stop
a little short of the
end of the board
and chisel away the
rest. This prevents
cutting the rabbet
around the corner
by mistake.*

Photo E: To make the tenons on the side rails, clamp the
two rails together and rout a rabbet on the top and
bottom.

Photo F: Rout the rabbets on the sides of the rails one at
a time. Be very careful not to run the bearing around the
end of the tenon when starting or finishing the cut.

Photo G: Drilling the hole for the bed bolt in the end of the rail is best done by using the post itself as a drill guide. Hold the post securely in place while you drill.

you're drilling. Since the holes are offset, you don't want to drill a rail offset the wrong way.

2. Drill down through the hole in the post as far as you can into the rail (see **photo G**). You'll have to drill deeper once you remove the post from the end of the rail to drill between 3½ in. and 4 in. deep, unless you have a very long twist drill to do the job all at once.

3. To drill holes in the longer side rails, clamp them in the bench vise at roughly a 45 degree angle. Otherwise, you'll have to climb up on a stepladder or on top of the bench itself to drill the hole.

Embedding the bed bolt nuts in the rails

Though traditional and elegant, capturing the nut for the bed bolt inside the rail is a lot of work and strictly an option. You could use any of the easier techniques described in the other projects in this book. But this technique leaves a completely hidden nut and eases bed assembly.

1. Rout a recess—basically a ½-in. by 1¾-in. by 1½-in.-deep mortise—on the inside face of the side rail (see "Setting a Captured Nut in the Rail").

2. Mill some tenon stock about 12 in. long, and round over the edges to match the rounded ends of the mortise (without glue).

3. Insert one end of the tenon stock all the way down into the mortise.

4. Insert a bed bolt into the hole in the end of the rail, and tap it to mark the bolt's location on the tenon stock.

5. Remove the tenon stock and lay out the location of the nut, centered around the bolt's mark.

6. Drill out the waste and carefully chisel the hole square so the nut fits snugly.

7. Put the nut in the square hole in the tenon stock and glue the stock in place (see **photo H**).

8. Thread the bolt onto the nut before the glue dries to be sure it works.

9. After the glue dries, cut the tenon flush with the inside rail. All that will show is a little patch of end grain.

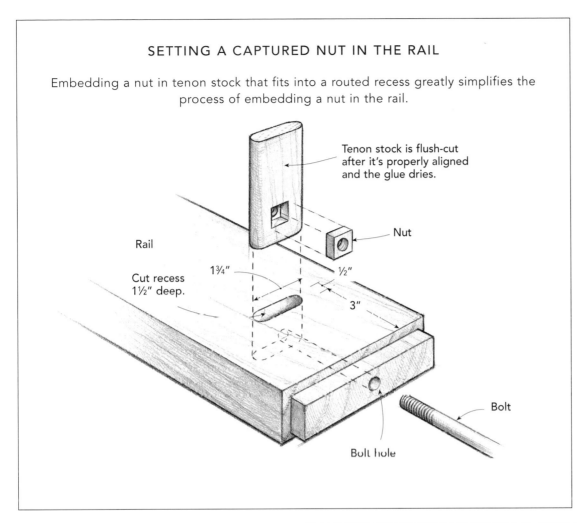

SETTING A CAPTURED NUT IN THE RAIL

Embedding a nut in tenon stock that fits into a routed recess greatly simplifies the process of embedding a nut in the rail.

Tenon stock is flush-cut after it's properly aligned and the glue dries.

Nut

Rail

Cut recess 1½" deep.

1¾"

½"

3"

Bolt

Bolt hole

Photo H: A captured nut is ready to be inserted into the mortise in the side rail. When glued in place and cut flush against the rail, it makes an elegant joint.

Adding the mattress hangers

To support the mattress, you can use special cast-iron mattress hangers, available from some of the specialty hardware catalogs listed in Sources on p. 183. You can also use full-length angle iron or ⅛-in. by 1½-in. by 1½-in. L-shaped aluminum angle stock. You could also use wooden cleats as in the First Bed project, but the metal brackets let you hide about 1 in. more of the box spring inside the rails.

1. Rout recesses for the cast-iron mattress hangers in the side rails so the box spring won't snag on the edges of the hardware. If you leave an extra ½-in. space between the rails, this won't be necessary.

2. Screw the hangers into place after all of the finishing for the bed has been done.

MAKING THE HEADBOARD

Gluing up the headboard

If you have a single board wide enough for the headboard without gluing it up, then skip to step 3. If not, you'll need to glue one up.

1. Choose the boards that will make up the headboard, making sure they match for color and grain. A board that is half the necessary width but twice the length is usually a good choice. That way you can cut it in half and have two boards very similar in character.

Photo I: Rout the tenon and the transition curve of the back of the headboard. Do this before you shape the headboard so the router fence can register against a long tenon edge.

2. Joint the edges carefully and glue together. Let the glued-up plank sit for at least 24 hours, and then smooth it.

3. Assemble the two headboard posts with the headboard rail to get an exact length for the headboard—don't just rely on the dimensions in the drawings for this.

4. Measure between the lower mortises on the posts; then add the depth of the mortises to come up with a final length for the headboard. Only then should you crosscut the headboard to length.

Cutting the tenons

The tenons on the headboard are not typical tenons in that there are no shoulders. Because the headboard is thicker than the mortises are wide, you do need to cut the edges of the headboard down to fit in the mortises. Although a straight taper can work, I recommend a curved transition.

1. Cut a 1⅛-in.-long rabbet across both ends of the back of the headboard, leaving just over the desired tenon thickness. This can be done on the table saw or by using a router and a straight bit with an auxiliary fence attached.

2. Draw the shape of the transition curve on an edge to guide your cuts.

3. With a core-box bit (a coving bit without a pilot) in the router, make a number of passes, adjusting both the fence and the bit height to waste away as much wood as possible (see **photo I**).

4. Scrape and sand the curve with sandpaper wrapped around a 1½-in.-diameter dowel to refine and smooth the shape of the transition (see **photo J**).

Shaping and fitting the headboard

1. Lay out an ellipse on the headboard (see "Headboard Details"), or draw out your own shape.

2. Bandsaw the headboard to shape. You'll need an assistant if you choose to bandsaw the oval cutouts on the sides of the headboard. You could cut these out with a jigsaw instead.

3. Sand all of the edges smooth, easing the corners slightly.

Photo J: Sand the routed curve thoroughly with a dowel block wrapped in sandpaper. The sanding is cross grain, but if you continue through 400 grit, it will look great.

HEADBOARD DETAILS

The headboard can have a simple or elliptical curve. The tenoned ends can be tapered or curved on the back side to fit into the post mortises.

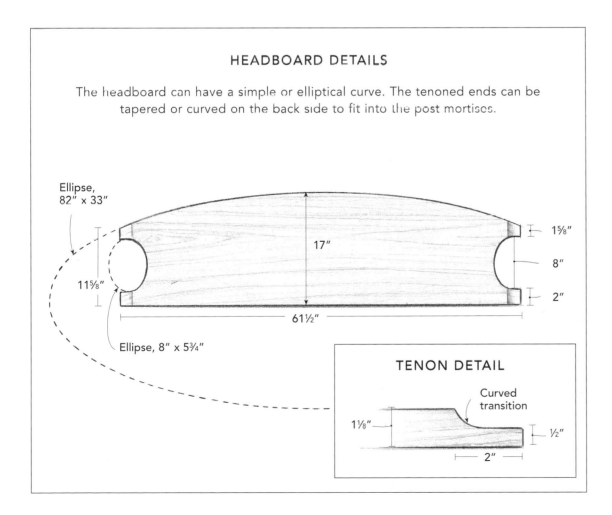

Ellipse, 82" x 33"

Ellipse, 8" x 5¾"

17"

11⅝"

1⅝"

8"

2"

61½"

TENON DETAIL

Curved transition

1⅛"

½"

2"

4. Plane, rasp, or sand the back sides of the tenons to fit in the mortises in the posts.

5. Smooth the curved transition out again if necessary after fitting the tenons.

6. Be sure to leave a little room for seasonal expansion and contraction of the headboard. The oval cutouts do not change the rules of wood movement.

FINISHING TOUCHES

Making the finials

Finials crown the tops of the bedposts and can be turned or carved to shape. They're optional but make a very nice detail that's worth the trouble. Or you can add a tester (see the details below).

1. Cut the turning blanks for the finials out of the same stock as the posts if you have any left. Though it's wasteful to cut 1⅝-in.-square blanks out of such thick stock, you'll have a close color match to the posts.

2. Make up a pattern to turn from in the same way described to turn the legs for the Shaker-Style Bed (see "Turning Patterns" on p. 44 and "Leg Turning Strategy" on p. 45).

3. Drill the ⅜-in.-diameter hole for the dowel pin before you turn the finial. A live center (a cone-shaped point with ball bearings in it so you don't have to worry about friction from the tailstock center) fits easily into this hole when setting up to turn.

4. Don't part off the narrow end of the finial until after you've finished sanding. Then take a final light touch with the point of a skew chisel to cut the waste off; the finial will drop free.

Making a tester

The tester (pronounced *teester*) is a wooden framework connecting the tops of the posts. It often has additional crosspieces between the side pieces. The tester is typically used instead of the finials.

1. Choose stock that is as straight as possible for the tester because the thin rails can warp easily over time. Mill the stock carefully for straightness.

2. To get the right lengths for the tester parts, assemble the entire bed first.

3. Measure from post to post on the outside, then subtract between ⅛ in. and ¼ in. in both directions. You may have to play with the numbers a little to come up with a rectangle. Putting the tester slightly under tension also helps to keep it straight.

4. Cut the tester parts to length and cut half-lap joints on the ends.

5. Hold a joint together snugly, then carefully drill through the center on a drill press.

6. Cut a facet on the corners of the tester to match the shape of the tops of the posts.

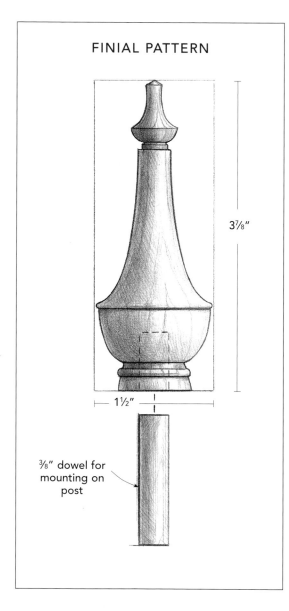

FINIAL PATTERN

3⅞"

1½"

⅜" dowel for mounting on post

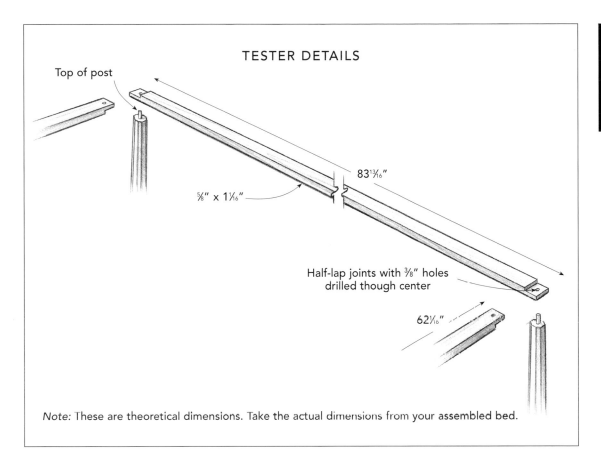

TESTER DETAILS

Top of post

⅝" x 1¹⁄₁₆"

83¹³⁄₁₆"

Half-lap joints with ⅜" holes
drilled though center

62¹⁄₁₆"

Note: These are theoretical dimensions. Take the actual dimensions from your assembled bed.

Tip: Smaller drill bits are less likely to wander when drilling into end grain.

Drilling the post tops for the finial or tester

1. Mark the exact centers of the tops of the posts by drawing the diagonals and marking their (approximate) intersection with an awl.

2. Lay the post on a workbench or long table, and clamp it in place. The benchtop provides a good reference for drilling straight down into the top of the post.

3. Drill a hole with a ¼-in. drill first, and check to see if the hole is centered. You get a chance to correct the hole location by enlarging the smaller hole a little bit before committing to the final size (see **photo K**).

4. Enlarge the hole to ⅜ in.

5. Mark and drill pilot holes for the screws for the bolt hole covers once all the finishing is done (see Appendix on p. 182 for finishing suggestions).

6. Hold the covers in place and tighten the screws until just barely snug. You should still be able to rotate the covers easily.

Photo K: To drill dowel holes for the finials, lay the posts down on a bench to guide your eye.

CITY BED

Sometimes the overall form of a bed makes the design interesting. The Windsor Bed (pp. 112-129) and the Sleigh Bed (pp. 144-163) are good examples of this. Other times it's the details that make the design. That's the case with the City Bed. The underlying form is very simple. The details transform this simple structure into a much more interesting bed. The structure doesn't appear simple at all once the legs have been transformed from square posts into columns with bases and little "temples" on top. And shaping the top edge of the headboard obscures the fact that it's essentially a simple rectangle.

This bed was inspired by the view of downtown Chicago from my wife's (then my girlfriend's) apartment. This is quite an abstraction, of course. The city doesn't look like this. But impressions of the local architecture along with highly distilled bits and pieces of various buildings found their way into the design. The profile of the headboard is an abstraction of the way several buildings look when bunched together at a distance. Only later did it occur to me that the overall design is reminiscent of some Arts and Crafts pieces.

The result is a bed with a lot of character and detail, but one that doesn't assault the eye with complexity. Much like a city skyline seen at a distance, there's a lot more going on than you can or really need to see right away to appreciate it.

City Bed

THIS IS A SIMPLE BED with rich details. Although the legs are the most complicated-looking parts of the bed, they are made up of fairly simple components. The capitals consist of rabbeted and dadoed square blocks. Only the pyramid top requires an off-square cut. The shaping of the headboard is the only other notable challenge, and this can be shaped with a router then squared up with a chisel.

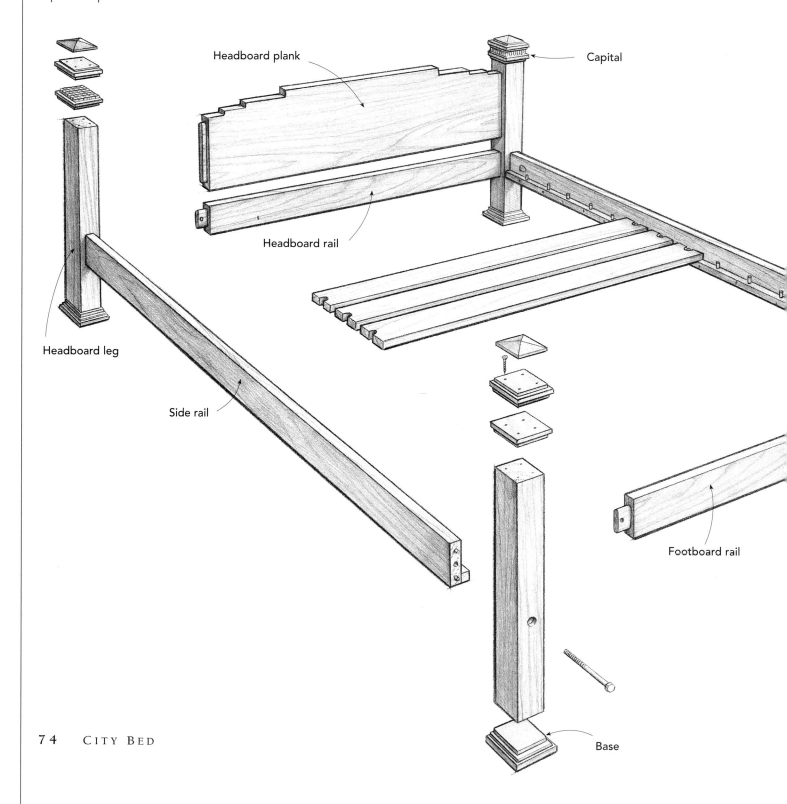

Headboard plank

Capital

Headboard rail

Headboard leg

Side rail

Footboard rail

Base

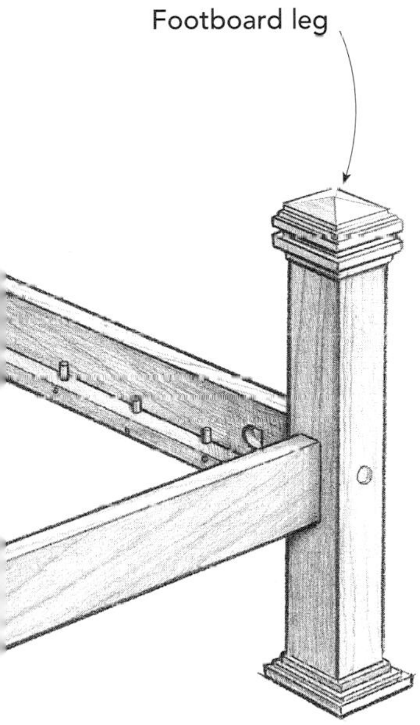

HEADBOARD

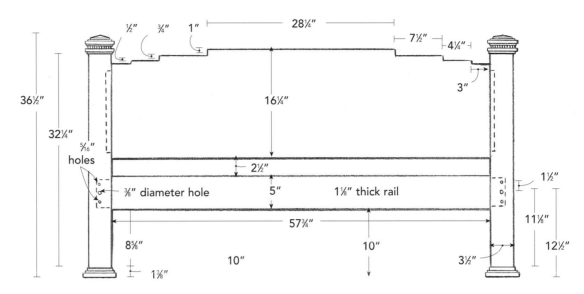

FOOTBOARD

Footboard leg

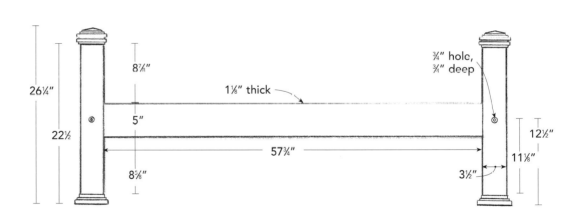

ADJUSTING FOR OTHER SIZE BEDS

(You may have to adjust heights based on mattress thickness; these dimensions are for a 6" to 8" thick mattress.)

	Footboard leg posts (excluding bases and caps)	Headboard leg posts (excluding bases and caps)	Headboard (plank) height	Width of headboard and footboard between rail tenons	Side rail length
King	Same as queen	34¾"	18¾"	73¾"	79½"
Double	Same as queen	32¼"	16¼"	51¾"	74½"

BUILDING THE BED STEP-BY-STEP

CUT LIST FOR CITY BED

Headboard and Footboard

2	Headboard legs	3½ in. x 3½ in. x 32¼ in.
2	Footboard legs	3½ in. x 3½ in. x 22½ in.
2	Headboard and footboard rails	1¹⁄₁₆ in. x 5 in. x 61¾ in.
1	Headboard plank	1⅛ in. x 16¼ in. x 58¾ in.

Bases and Capitals

2	Capital tops (A)	3¼ in. x 3¼ in. x ¾ in.
4	Capital midsections (B)	4½ in. x 4½ in. x 1 in.
2	Headboard capital bottom sections (C)	4½ in. x 4½ in. x 1¼ in.
2	Footboard capital bottom sections (D)	4½ in. x 4½ in. x ¾ in.
4	Bases (E)	5 in. x 5 in. x 1⅜ in.

Side Rails

2	Side rails	1¹⁄₁₆ in. x 5 in. x 80 in.
2	Cleats	1 in. x 1¼ in. x 80 in.
16	Slats	¾ in. x 4 in. x 60⅛ in.

Hardware

4	Hex-head bolts with washers and nuts	⁵⁄₁₆ in. x 6 in.
2	Drywall screws	#8 x 3 in.
32	Dowel pins	⁵⁄₁₆ in. x 1¼ in.
8	Drywall screws, fine-threaded	#6 x 2 in.
8	Drywall screws, fine-threaded	#6 x 2½ in.
8	Drywall screws, fine-threaded	#8 x 3 in.
	#6 x 2½ in. screws, as needed	

These dimensions are for a queen-size bed. You may have to adjust your dimensions to suit the bed size, the mattress size, or any differences in wood dimensions.

THE BED CONSTRUCTION is straightforward and follows the pattern set up in the First Bed. You should refer back to that project for a more detailed discussion of the construction basics (see pp. 18-35). Much of the discussion here focuses on the specifics of making the bases and capitals for the legs and on shaping the headboard.

MAKING THE LEGS

Gluing up the leg blanks

The easiest way to make the legs is to mill them out of 16/4 lumber. But chunks of wood like this are not always easy to find. Gluing up 8/4 stock is the best compromise. The glued-up blanks need to be 4 in. wide and about 1 in. longer than the final dimensions required (see "Gluing Up a Thick Leg").

1. Spread glue evenly over one of the faces, and clamp the blanks together.
2. Use a lot of clamps so that the pressure is evenly spread over the entire leg. Wait at least 24 hours for the glue to dry.
3. Plane or rip the legs to 3½ in. by 3½ in.
4. Cut the legs to length.

Drilling for the bed bolts

1. Mark the location for the bed bolt hole with a sharp awl 11⅛ in. up from the bottom of the leg and centered from side to side. Mark all legs on both sides.
2. Drill first from the outside with a ¾-in. bit, going roughly ¾ in. deep. This is the counterbore hole.
3. Drill in the center of this hole with a ⅜-in. bit, going about halfway through the leg.

GLUING UP A THICK LEG

When you don't have stock thick enough to mill the legs, gluing them up from two pieces is the best option.

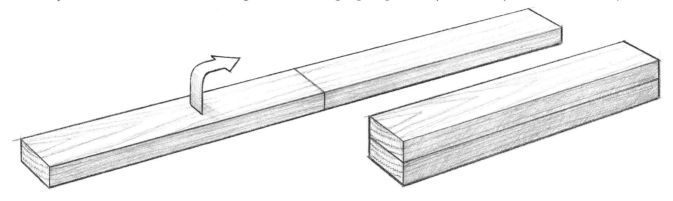

Cut a longer board in half, and slide one half on the top of the other to get a good match of grain direction and appearance. Avoid gluing separate pieces with different grain. The unlike wood movement will break down the joint.

4. Flip the leg over, and drill with the ⅜-in. bit until the holes meet up. This way, if the bit wanders at all when cutting through the 3½ in. of leg, it won't throw off the location.
5. Drill the two ⁵⁄₁₆-in. alignment holes using the jig described in "A Bolt Hole Drilling Guide" on p. 28. The work can also be done by carefully marking and drilling on a drill press.

Cutting the leg mortises

The headboard and footboard rails fit into a ½-in.-thick, 2-in.-deep, 3-in.-wide mortise in the legs.

1. Lay out the mortises centered and between 9⅝ in. and 12⅝ in. up from the bottom of the leg (see "Headboard Leg Joinery Details" on p. 78).
2. Cut the mortises for the headboard plank 16⅝ in. to 29⅝ in. up from the bottom. These mortises are also ½ in. wide but are only ⁹⁄₁₆ in. deep. A plunge router with a fence attached does the job easily.

Drilling pilot holes for the headboard pins

1. Lay out the pilot holes for the pins on both the outside and inside. Measure carefully so the holes line up.
2. On a drill press, drill from the inside with a ³⁄₁₆-in. drill bit in the center of the headboard mortise halfway through the leg.
3. Drill in from the outside with a ⅛-in. bit until the two holes connect.

Milling the rails

1. Mill the headboard, footboard, and side rails to 1⅛ in. thick. Presurfaced 5/4 lumber will be 1¹⁄₁₆ in. thick and is fine to use. Your mattress will have an extra ⅛ in. of space if you don't adjust the length of the headboard and footboard rails.
2. Tenon both ends of the footboard rail, but cut only one end on the headboard rail for now. You'll cut the opposite end after the headboard plank is done, so the lengths can be exactly the same.

Tip: Mark the tops of each leg for future reference. It's not always obvious which end is up on the footboard, where the joinery is almost (but not quite) in the center of the leg.

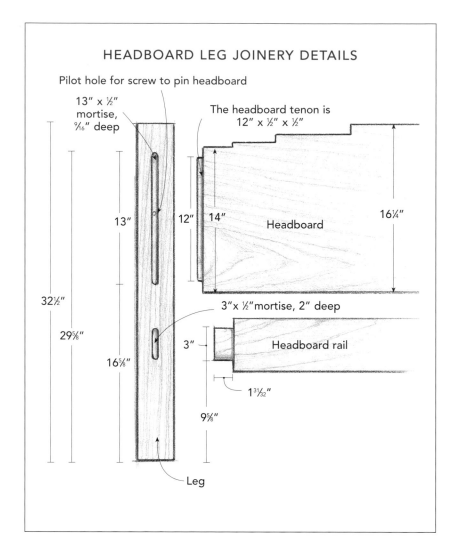

HEADBOARD LEG JOINERY DETAILS

Pilot hole for screw to pin headboard

13" x ½" mortise, ⁹⁄₁₆" deep

The headboard tenon is 12" x ½" x ½"

13"

12"

14"   Headboard

16¼"

32½"

29⅝"

3" x ½" mortise, 2" deep

3"   Headboard rail

16⅝"

1³¹⁄₃₂"

9⅝"

Leg

---

3. Cut the $1^{31}/_{32}$-in. by 3-in. tenons. I use the jig described in "A Tenoning Jig" on p. 24.

4. Plane or rasp the tenons if necessary to get a tight fit in their mortises.

5. Mark each tenon for its specific mortise. This will also make it clear which ones you've done already.

Making the headboard plank

When gluing up the headboard plank, it's important to use wood from the same board. Try to place the seam down the middle. Unfortunately you can't just cut the headboard to length as a perfect rectangle. It helps to make the headboard slightly wider at the top, by about $1/32$ in. This eliminates the seemingly inevitable gap that forms between the headboard and the legs.

1. Glue up the headboard plank. After it's dry, smooth it by planing, scraping, and sanding as necessary.

2. Rip the headboard to overall width.

3. Decide how you want to orient the headboard, and mark the top clearly.

4. Set up a crosscut tray with an added 2-in.-wide, 1-in.-thick auxiliary fence. You want the auxiliary fence to be longer than the headboard plank and set so the blade will cut through it. The kerf will help you line up the cut on the other side (see "Cutting the Headboard Plank to Width").

5. Place the bottom edge of the headboard against the fence,

6. Add a $1/32$-in.-thick shim between the fence and the headboard, about 1 in. away from the blade, and cut one edge. This should give you the correct amount of splay to keep the upper part of the headboard shoulder tight against the leg.

7. Flip the headboard over so that the bottom is still against the fence, shim it, and carefully measure from the opposite end of the headboard on the edge that's against the auxiliary fence (the bottom). Your measurement should be 1 in. longer than the intended shoulder-to-shoulder length of the headboard rail.

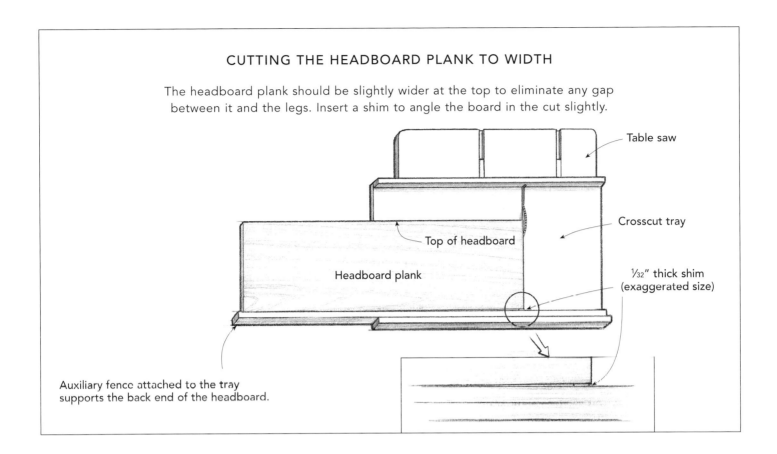

CUTTING THE HEADBOARD PLANK TO WIDTH

The headboard plank should be slightly wider at the top to eliminate any gap
between it and the legs. Insert a shim to angle the board in the cut slightly.

Table saw

Crosscut tray

Top of headboard

Headboard plank

1/32" thick shim
(exaggerated size)

Auxiliary fence attached to the tray
supports the back end of the headboard.

8. Line up your mark with the edge of the kerf in the auxiliary fence. It shows exactly where the blade will cut.

Tenoning the headboard plank

To make the tenons on the ends of the headboard plank, simply cut rabbets on both sides of both ends.

1. On one end of the headboard, mark out the thickness of the tenon centered on the edge.
2. Set up a router with a 1/2-in. rabbeting bit to cut a tenon slightly over 1/2 in. thick.
3. Clamp a piece of scrap at the far side of the headboard to prevent tearout on that edge. Don't worry about tearout at the top of the headboard because it will be cut away when you cut the headboard profile.
4. Rout both faces of each end of the headboard.
5. Saw away the waste on top and bottom of the tenons. Pare the stub away with a 3/4-in.-wide chisel.

6. Test-fit the tenons. If they are too tight, trim them to size with a shoulder plane, a rasp held flat on the cheeks, or some sandpaper on a block. Rasps and sandpaper tend to leave the area near the shoulder a little thicker than the rest of the tenon, and you'll have to pare this flush with a chisel.
7. Go back and finish tenoning the headboard rail. Use the bottom edge of the headboard—the top is about 1/32 in. wider—as a ruler to mark out the exact length of the rail between the tenons, then cut and fit the tenon to the leg mortise.

Cutting the headboard profile

Shaping the top of the headboard is best done with a router and template. This will leave a clean edge with only the corners to square up. To do this you need to make a routing template as shown in "Headboard Routing Template" on p. 80.

Tip: Don't try to crosscut the headboard plank to width on the table saw with just a miter gauge. The large board will be almost impossible to control. Use a crosscut tray.

Headboard Routing Template

BUILDING THE JIG

1. Rip strips of 1", ¾", and ½" off of one edge of a piece of ½" thick hardwood about 7" wide by 40" long.
2. Lay out the strips and board, marking where each will go, and glue them together.
3. Cut off the protruding ends, and plane or sand both sides of the template smooth once the glue has dried.

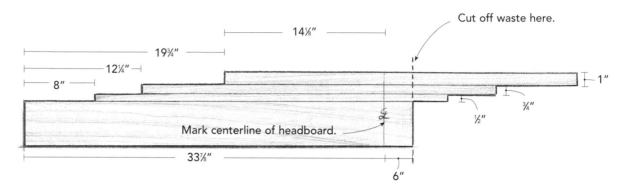

14⅛"
19¾"
12¼"
8"
1"
¾"
½"
Cut off waste here.
Mark centerline of headboard.
33⅞"
6"

HEADBOARD PROFILE DIMENSIONS

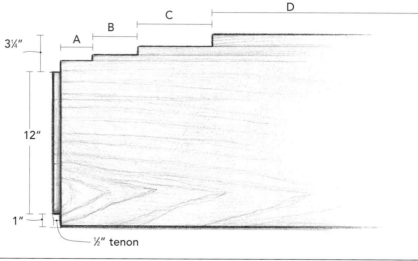

3¼"
12"
1"
½" tenon
A B C D

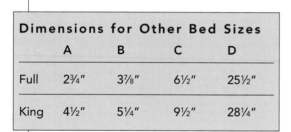

Dimensions for Other Bed Sizes				
	A	**B**	**C**	**D**
Full	2¾"	3⅞"	6½"	25½"
King	4½"	5¼"	9½"	28¼"

1. Place the template on the headboard so that the uppermost step is 14¾ in. from the edge.

2. Trace the template onto the headboard.

3. Flip the template over and mark the other side. Depending on your bandsaw, you may have to mark out the shape for half the headboard on the back side.

4. Cut most of the waste on the bandsaw within 1/16 in. of the line.

5. Reposition the template on the front of the headboard and on the right side as you would see it from the footboard. This will allow you to rout in the proper direction.

6. Clamp the template in place, with the center marks aligned and the top edge flush with the top of the headboard.

7. Set up the router with a straight pattern bit, which has a ball-bearing pilot above the cutter, and rout the profile flush with the template.

8. Rout the other side from the back of the board.

9. To cut the routed corners square, use a sharp chisel. First pare across the grain to get rid of the bulk of the waste. Work from both sides so you don't split off any wood (see **photo A**).

Photo A: To pare the headboard detail corners square, first work horizontally from both sides to the middle, so you don't chip off any wood by paring over the opposite edge. Watch those fingers!

10. For the finish cuts, work down from the top first (see **photo B**). Then carefully work in horizontally. Use a sweeping cut with the flat side of the chisel riding on the surface and the handle off to one side.

11. Once all the corners have been squared up, scrape and sand the edges flat and smooth.

12. Ease or lightly chamfer all the edges on the headboard.

13. File or chisel all the chamfers so that they meet at a 45 degree angle.

Gluing up the headboard and footboard

1. Spread glue in the footboard mortises and very lightly on the tenons, then assemble the joints.

2. Clamp the joint with a clamp on each side and slightly offset from each other.

3. Spread glue in the headboard rail mortise, and lightly on the rail tenon, but don't put any glue in the long mortise for the headboard plank.

Photo B: Next, hold the chisel firmly against the vertical part of the step and pare down. Take off only a small amount of wood at a time.

4. Put the rail into one leg, then insert the headboard plank. Then put the other leg on and clamp the rail as you did for the footboard.

5. Check the distance between the rail and the headboard to make sure the headboard is lined up properly.

6. Then clamp across the top of the legs to hold the headboard in place and drive #8 by 3-in. drywall screws into the countersunk pilot holes in the legs to pin the headboard in place (see "Tricks for Driving Screws").

7. When the screws are tight and the legs are snug against the headboard, plug the pilot holes, and trim and sand the plugs flush with the legs.

8. Because the tenons now plug up the bolt holes in the legs, redrill them with a ⅜-in. bit.

TIPS FOR DRIVING SCREWS

Most of the time, I use an electric drill fitted with a Phillips or a square-drive tip to drive screws. This is both fast and easy, but it's easy to snap the heads off the screws. I rely on two simple precautions to avoid this frustration: drilling proper pilot holes and lubricating the screws.

Pilot holes should be properly sized for the screws you're using. There are two different types of pilot hole to consider as well: the hole that the threads will bite into (the anchor hole), and the hole that the screw will go through without the threads catching (the shank hole). This hole is what allows the screw to pull parts together.

The pilot for the anchor hole should be the same size as the root diameter (the part inside the threads) of the screw. The shank hole must be larger than the diameter of the threads. I may not always drill an anchor hole—drywall screws drive themselves in quite well without one—but I always drill a shank hole.

And I always use either soap or wax to lubricate the screws.

MAKING THE CAPITALS AND BASES

Milling the parts for the capitals and bases

The capitals are complicated looking, but they just use rabbeted parts to create the whole. All of the cutting can be done on the router table, except for the columns in part C, which are best cut on the table saw. "Capitals and Bases" shows how the parts go together.

1. Mill the various blanks for the capitals and bases to size. Make some extras in case something goes awry—especially of part C, which has all of the columns.

2. Cut all of the ¼-in. by ¼-in. crossgrain rabbets, then the rabbets with the grain, in parts B, C, and D. This minimizes tearout at the end of the cut.

3. Reset the router to make the ¼-in. by ⅜-in. rabbet on the top of part B, and then to make the ½-in. by ⅝-in. rabbets and the ¾-in. by ¼-in. rabbets in part E (see **photo C** on p. 84).

4. Sand all of the rabbets now to get rid of the saw or router marks. Don't sand the tops of any of the B parts or the top of the D parts, since these are glue surfaces and must be as flat as possible. Don't bother to sand any of the outside edges, since you'll sand these after you've glued the capitals together.

Cutting the columns for part C

The columns on the capitals, part C, are cut with a series of dado cuts on the table saw (see **photo D** on p. 84).

1. Cut a ½-in. by ¼-in. rabbet around the top edge on the router table.

2. Set up the table saw with a ⁵⁄₁₆-in. dado blade.

3. Mark out the location of the ⁵⁄₁₆-in. dado in the center of the piece.

4. Mill up three strips, ⅝ in. thick by 1¼ in. wide by 24 in. long, to register the cuts for all of the columns. The thickness of these strips (in conjunction with a ⁵⁄₁₆-in. dado cutter)

Capitals and Bases

For each bed you'll need 4 A parts, 4 B parts, 2 C parts for the headboard legs, 2 D parts for footboard legs, and 4 E parts for the leg bases.

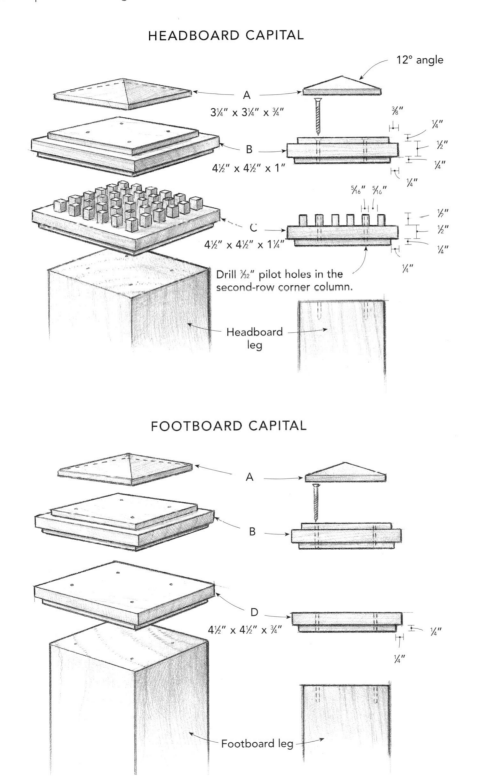

HEADBOARD CAPITAL

12° angle

A

3¼" x 3¼" x ¾"

B

4½" x 4½" x 1"

⅜"

¼"

½"

¼"

¼"

C

4½" x 4½" x 1¼"

⁵⁄₁₆" ⁵⁄₁₆"

½"

½"

¼"

¼"

Drill ³⁄₃₂" pilot holes in the second-row corner column.

Headboard leg

FOOTBOARD CAPITAL

A

B

D

4½" x 4½" x ¾"

¼"

¼"

Footboard leg

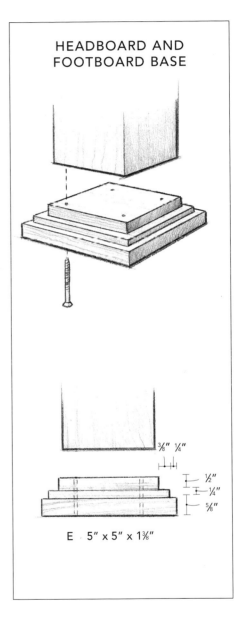

HEADBOARD AND FOOTBOARD BASE

⅜" ¼"

½"

¼"

⁵⁄₈"

E · 5" x 5" x 1⅜"

Photo C: A router table setup works well for cutting the rabbets in the base and capital parts.

will create ⁵⁄₁₆-in. columns. If your dado set cuts a different-size groove, you'll have to adjust the strip thickness. The strips make it easy to keep all of the columns exactly the same size.

5. Clamp the three strips to the fence, leaving enough room both in front of and behind the blade for safety.

6. Set the fence (with the strips attached) so that the blade will cut exactly in the center, and make the first cut across the grain on all pieces.

7. Remove one of the ⅝-in.-thick strips from the fence, then make the next pair of across-the-grain cuts.

8. Rotate the piece 180 degrees and, with the same fence setting, cut the third dado across the grain (see **photo E**). Repeat these cuts on all of the pieces.

9. Continue in this way with the remaining crossgrain cuts, removing the second and then the third strips (see **photo F**).

10. Clamp the strips back onto the fence, and make all of the rip cuts in exactly the same way. You should wind up with a perfect set of columns.

11. Drill four ³⁄₃₂-in. holes in the second-row corner columns (just one in from the edges) (see **photo G** on p. 86). These will serve as pilot holes later on when you attach the capi-

Photo D: This is the sequence of table-saw dado cuts that will produce the columns for the headboard capital part C.

Photo E: Strips clamped to the fence align the dado cuts in the column part. Here, I have removed one strip to cut the second and third dadoes.

tals to the columns. If you run into trouble with columns snapping off, you can put some 5/16-in. strips in between the rows to support them while you're drilling. A sharp drill bit helps, too.

Assembling the capitals

To assemble the various parts into well-aligned capitals, first make a quick jig (see "Capital Clamping Jig" on p. 86).

1. When gluing up a footboard capital, spread a small amount of glue in the center of the bottom of part B, then align and clamp it to part D in the jig.

2. For a headboard capital, put a very small spot of glue on top of each of the columns on part C, including the columns with the holes, then align it and clamp it to part B in the jig (see **photo H** on p. 86).

3. When the glue is dry, sand the edges of the capitals on a stationary belt sander or by hand to smooth them and remove any slight misalignment. Ease the edges and corners slightly with some 220-grit sandpaper.

Photo F: Removing a strip lets you cut the next series of dadoes. I still have to remove this strip to cut the outsides of the outermost columns.

Tip: Remember that grain direction should match on all of the capital parts.

Photo G: Drill ³⁄₃₂-in. pilot holes in the second-row corner columns on a drill press slowly and carefully. I eyeball the center on each of the columns.

Photo H: Place a set of capital parts into the jig with a scrap on top as a pad, and clamp.

CAPITAL CLAMPING JIG

This simple jig ensures that the capital parts are clamped together in alignment. To make the jig, attach some pieces of scrap to three sides of an extra blank for one of the 4½" square parts, or make the jig from scratch.

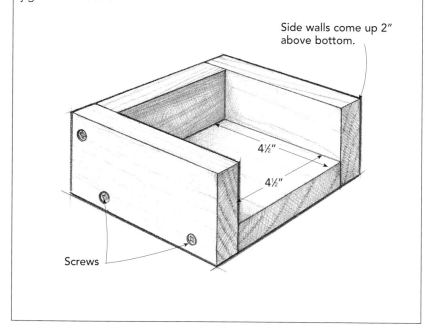

Side walls come up 2" above bottom.

4½"

4½"

Screws

Attaching the base and capitals to the legs

1. Drill four pilot holes in the footboard capitals, and countersink them on the top, making sure that the holes and countersinks are within the area that will be covered by the pyramid top.

2. For the headboard capitals, you have to drill very slowly and carefully with progressively larger bits (⅛ in., ⁵⁄₃₂ in., ³⁄₁₆ in.) through the ³⁄₃₂-in. pilot holes you've already drilled in the columns. Use a drill press to be sure you're drilling absolutely straight. Then countersink the holes from the top.

3. Line up a base or capital with the grain running from side to side on the bed, centered on the leg (see **photo I**).

4. Screw in just one of the screws (see **photo J**). Use 2-in. fine-thread drywall screws for the base, 2½ in. fine-thread drywall screws for the footboard capitals, and 3-in. fine-thread drywall screws for the headboard capitals.

5. With one of the screws in, check to be sure the leg is still centered on the piece, then screw in the rest. If you have to adjust the position, you can remove the first screw and try again in one of the other pilot holes.

Photo I: Center the capital on the leg. You can measure or just eyeball.

Making and attaching the pyramids

The pyramid on top of the columns, part A, must be cut carefully so that all of the lines intersect with the corners and at the center. You need to build a simple table-saw jig to achieve this level of accuracy. (see **photo K** on p. 88 and "Pyramid-Cutting Jig" on p. 89).

1. Cut the pyramids on the table saw with the jig.

2. Place a sheet of sandpaper on a flat surface and carefully stroke each facet of the pyramid to sand them smooth without distorting the shape. Inspect the pyramid often to make sure you're not oversanding one of the facets (see **photo L** on p. 88). Sand the thin vertical edges as well.

3. To attach the pyramids, mark out a set of lines just inside where the pyramid will actually go on top of the column.

4. Spread a thin layer of glue around all but the outside ½ in. of the underside of the pyramid, and press it into place, with the grain of the pyramid aligned with the grain of the rest of the capital. Just hold the piece on the right place for a minute or two until the glue tacks up.

Photo J: Hold the capital carefully in place, then screw it down. Before you drive the second screw, be sure the capital hasn't shifted.

Tip: Screwing into end grain is known for weakness, but it works well here because there is very little stress on the screws.

Photo K: The pyramid-cutting jig makes it safe and easy to cut perfect pyramids.

Photo L: Sanding the pyramids smooth takes a careful touch. Place the sandpaper on a flat surface and draw the pyramid slowly and carefully over it.

Photo M: Secure the glued pyramid to the column top with rubber strips cut from an inner tube or with strong elastic bands.

5. Wrap rubber straps cut out of a bicycle inner tube or even strong rubber bands to hold the pyramid down (see **photo M**). Be sure the pyramids don't shift off center.

MAKING THE SIDE RAILS AND MATTRESS SUPPORTS

Making the side rails

The side rails are identical to those on the First Bed, except for their size.

1. Mill up the side rails if you haven't already done so.

2. Cut them to length. Because of the thickness of the legs, these rails should be ½ in. shorter than the mattress length.

3. Drill the bolt and guide holes and rout the nut recess exactly as described in the First Bed (see p. 32). Use ⁵⁄₁₆-in. by 6-in. hex-head bolts with washers and nuts.

Making the cleats and slats

The cleats and slats are also the same as on the First Bed, though you do have other choices (see "Metal Mattress Supports").

PYRAMID-CUTTING JIG

This jig guides the blank through the cut, ensuring accuracy and a point at the top of the pyramid.

Wedge

Clamp bar

Screw and washer in oversize hole in clamp bar

Screws recessed below surface

3¼"

Pyramid blank

Slot sized to fit rip fence

⁷⁄₃₂"

¼" plywood tacked to bottom

Clamp bar

Wedge

Rip fence

Blank

Blade

Table saw

1. Mill 1-in. by 1¼-in. strips of whatever wood you have handy.

2. Drill for ⁵⁄₁₆-in. dowel pins that stick up to register the slats.

3. Screw them to the insides of the side rails.

4. Mill the slats out of maple to ¾ in. by 4 in., sized to fit between the rails and notched so they can slip over the pins in the cleats.

FINISHING UP

There's only one unusual aspect to finishing this bed: The inside columns on the headboard capital are hard to reach. I squirt oil in between the columns, then spray it around with some compressed air. You could also blow forcefully into a soda straw directed in the same way. Fortunately, you don't have to worry about sanding in there. Otherwise, choose your finish and have at it (see Appendix on p. 182 for finishing suggestions).

METAL MATTRESS SUPPORTS

Box springs do not need slats to support them, just cleats. You can still make them out of wood, but you have metal options, including cast-iron mattress hangers as for the Pencil-Post Bed, or 1¼-in. channel iron. These metal hangers also let the box spring sit a little lower, allowing you to conceal a little more of the box spring inside the side rails.

I've found that L-shaped extruded aluminum is easier to work with than the iron, but both function well and are available at most hardware stores. These metal mattress hangers are not less work. Cutting the channel stock to length, then drilling, countersinking, and deburring the holes in metal takes a while. But it does reduce the overall bulk of the bed and can compensate for a mattress that is a little thicker than average.

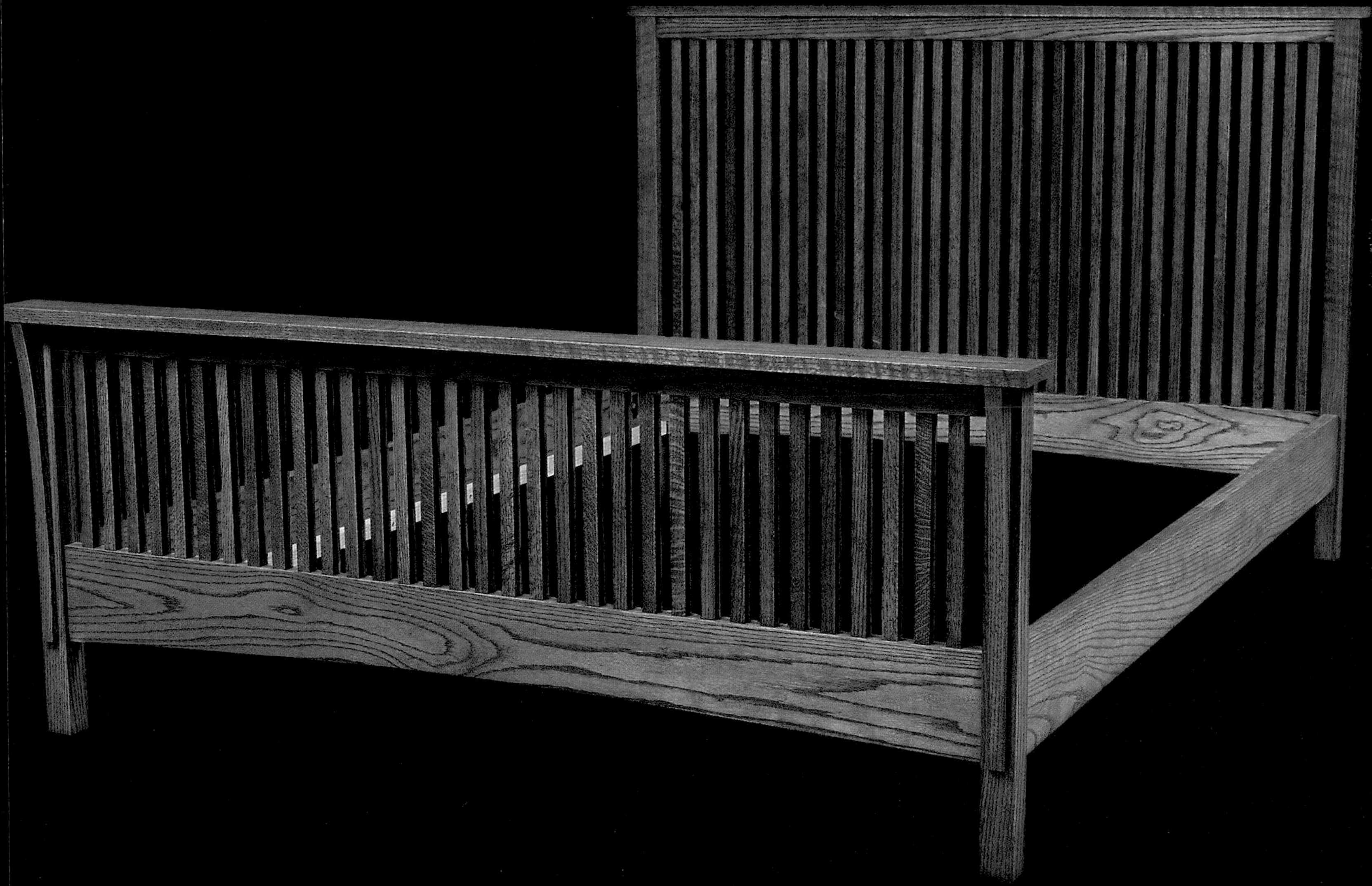

CRAFTSMAN-STYLE BED

The design of the Craftsman-Style Bed should be pretty familiar. There are currently many Craftsman-inspired designs similar to this in furniture stores and catalogs, a reflection of the popularity of the style.

My design does not come from a specific bed of the Craftsman period. In fact, I took most of the details from a Stickley design for a settee. I liked the settee and thought it would work well as a bed. Most of the original Stickley beds had fewer, wider slats and tall legs that extended up past the upper rails of the bed. Interestingly, these beds also had iron side rails that were not meant to be seen—they were normally concealed by the bedspread or covers.

Most Craftsman-style furniture was made of white oak with a rich brown finish created by fuming with ammonia. But this bed looks good in other woods as well. I chose to make the bed in oak, but I stained the wood with a medium-walnut-colored penetrating oil and varnish finish. The dark stain makes the grain patterns prominent.

I like a gentle curve on the bottom edge of the footboard rail. It lightens up the piece a little and, with the curve of the "wings" on the legs, relieves the otherwise overwhelming dominance of straight lines. If there is any chance that the bed will wind up with the headboard end showing, you should curve the bottom edge of the headboard rail as well.

Craftsman-Style Bed

CONTEMPLATING ALL OF THE SLATS may be a little overwhelming, but you don't really have to cut mortises for all of them (unless you want to) The combination of grooves in the rails and dentil strip fillers makes the mortises easily. Note that the bed bolt nuts are hidden by the wings on the outsides of the legs.

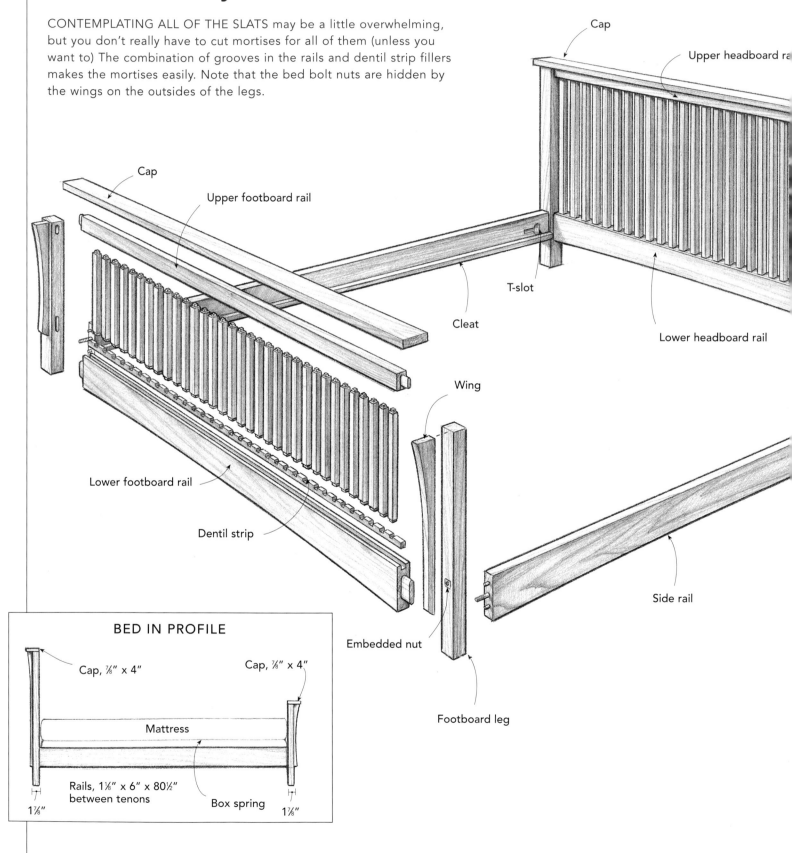

Cap

Upper headboard ra[il]

Cap

Upper footboard rail

T-slot

Cleat

Lower headboard rail

Wing

Lower footboard rail

Dentil strip

Embedded nut

Side rail

Footboard leg

BED IN PROFILE

Cap, ⅞" x 4"

Cap, ⅞" x 4"

Mattress

Rails, 1⅛" x 6" x 80½" between tenons

Box spring

1⅞"

1⅞"

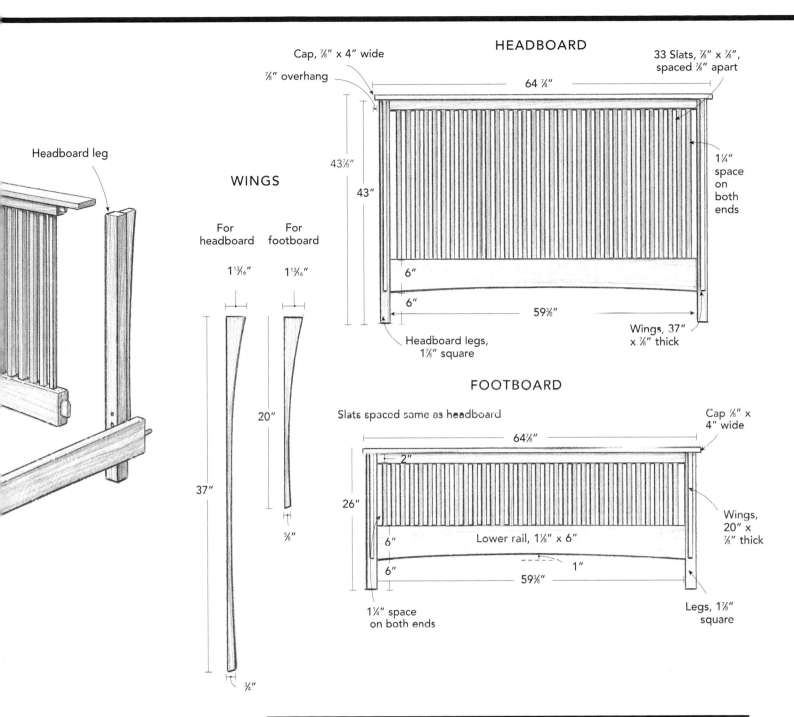

HEADBOARD

Cap, ⅞" x 4" wide

⅞" overhang

33 Slats, ⅞" x ⅞", spaced ⅞" apart

64⅞"

43⅞"

43"

1¼" space on both ends

6"

6"

59⅜"

Headboard legs, 1⅞" square

Wings, 37" x ⅞" thick

WINGS

For headboard

For footboard

1¹³⁄₁₆"

1¹³⁄₁₆"

20"

37"

⅝"

¾"

Headboard leg

FOOTBOARD

Slats spaced same as headboard

Cap ⅞" x 4" wide

64⅞"

2"

26"

6"

6"

Lower rail, 1⅛" x 6"

1"

59⅜"

Wings, 20" x ⅞" thick

Legs, 1⅞" square

1¼" space on both ends

RAIL LENGTHS FOR OTHER BED SIZES

	Twin	Full	King
For headboard and footboard	38⅜"	53⅜"	75⅜"
For side rail	75½"	75½"	80½"

All measurements are between tenons.

BUILDING THE BED STEP-BY-STEP

CUT LIST FOR CRAFTSMAN-STYLE BED

Headboard and Footboard

2	Headboard legs	1⅞ in. x 1⅞ in. x 43 in.
2	Footboard legs	1⅞ in. x 1⅞ in. x 26 in.
2	Headboard/footboard rails	1⅛ in. x 6 in. x 62⁹⁄₁₆ in.
2	Upper headboard/footboard rails	1⅛ in. x 2 in. x 62⁹⁄₁₆ in.
4	Dentil strips	½ in. x ½ in. x 59⅜ in.
33	Headboard slats	⅞ in. x ⅞ in. x 29¹¹⁄₁₆ in.
33	Footboard slats	⅞ in. x ⅞ in. x 12¹¹⁄₁₆ in.
2	Caps	⅞ in. x 4 in. x 64⅞ in.
2	Headboard wings	⅞ in. x 2½ in. x 37 in.
2	Footboard wings	⅞ in. x 2½ in. x 20 in.

Side Rails

2	Side rails	1⅛ in. by 6 in. x 80½ in.
2	Cleats	1 in. x 1¼ in. x 79⅞ in.

Hardware

4	Bed bolts	⁵⁄₁₆ in. x 5½ in.
8	Dowels (for alignment pins)	⁵⁄₁₆ in. x 1¼ in.

#6 x 2½-in. screws, as needed

These dimensions are for a queen-size bed with a box spring and mattress that have a combined thickness of up to 17 in. or 18 in. You may have to adjust your dimensions to suit the bed size, the mattress size, or any differences in wood dimensions.

Tip: Square pieces with end grain running diagonally will usually have straight grain on all four sides. This is sometimes called rift sawn.

THE CRAFTSMAN-STYLE BED takes us into some new but not unfamiliar territory. The most different aspect is the slatted headboard and footboard. This queen-size bed has 66 slats, 33 in both the headboard and the footboard. A less obvious difference is the bed-rail joinery system. The bed is bolted together, even though there are no visible bolt holes on the outside. The bolts go on the inside, with nuts embedded in the outsides of the legs, covered by the wings. The dimensions given are for a queen-size bed.

MILLING PARTS FOR THE HEADBOARD AND FOOTBOARD

Making the legs

1. Choose wood for the four legs that's straight grained on all four sides. This isn't critical, but it looks nice.
2. Mill the four 1⅞-in.-square legs, and cut them to length. Make sure that the legs are square. If they aren't, you'll have problems with the joinery later.
3. Lay out the locations for the mortises (see "Headboard and Footboard Joinery Details"). Use the bottom of the legs as a reference point when cutting the lower rail mortises, and use the tops of the legs when cutting mortises for the upper rails.
4. Cut the mortises however you prefer. I use the jig described in "Mortising Jig for Routing Thin Workpieces" on p. 23.

Making the rails

1. Mill the wood for all of the rails at one time, including the lower and upper headboard and footboard rails and the side rails. Choose the best grain for the footboard rail because it's the one you'll see most.

Headboard and Footboard Joinery Details

The upper and lower rails are the same on the headboard and footboard.

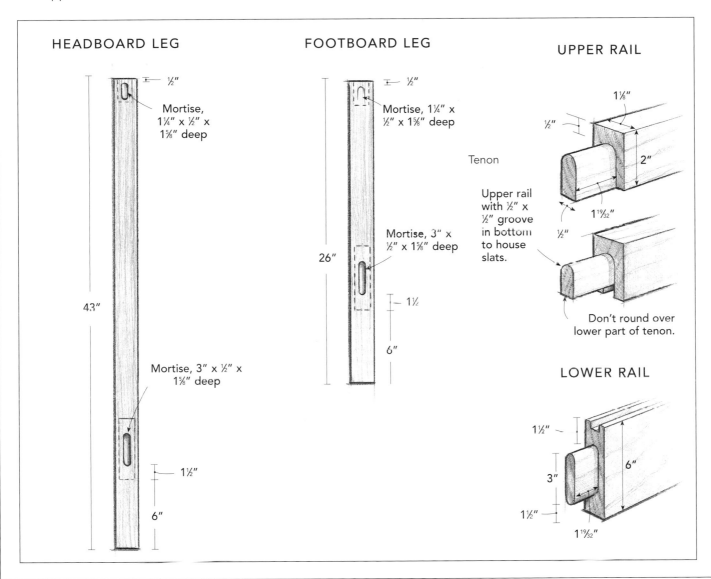

HEADBOARD LEG

Mortise, 1¼" x ½" x 1⅝" deep

½"

43"

Mortise, 3" x ½" x 1⅝" deep

1½"

6"

FOOTBOARD LEG

Mortise, 1¼" x ½" x 1⅝" deep

½"

26"

Mortise, 3" x ½" x 1⅝" deep

1½

6"

UPPER RAIL

1⅛"

½"

2"

1¹⁹⁄₃₂"

Tenon

½"

Upper rail with ½" x ½" groove in bottom to house slats.

Don't round over lower part of tenon.

LOWER RAIL

1½"

3"

1½"

6"

1¹⁹⁄₃₂"

2. Rip the lower headboard and footboard rails and the side rails to 6 in. wide, and rip the upper headboard and footboard rails to 2 in. wide.

Tenoning the rails

1. Cut the tenons with the tenoning jig described in the First Bed, or however else you prefer. For tenon layout, see "Headboard and Footboard Joinery Details."

2. Cut all of the lower rail tenons before moving on to the uppers.

3. Cut the tenon on one side of the upper rail and mark the second shoulder location on the upper rail directly from the lower rail (see "Matching Upper Rail and Lower Rail Length" on p. 96). This technique ensures that the distance between shoulders is the same on both headboard and footboard rails and especially between the upper and lower rails.

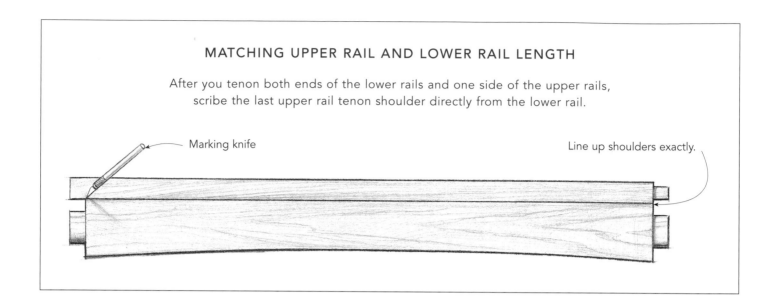

MATCHING UPPER RAIL AND LOWER RAIL LENGTH

After you tenon both ends of the lower rails and one side of the upper rails,
scribe the last upper rail tenon shoulder directly from the lower rail.

Marking knife

Line up shoulders exactly.

LEAVING OUT LAYOUT LINES

When you lay out joinery, it's often tempting to draw every line that describes each joint on every piece. However, you can save a lot of time if you lay out only the lines you really need. And this depends largely on the methods you use to cut the joints.

If you use a chisel to chop a mortise, or a handsaw (or a bandsaw) to cut a tenon by eye, you'll need exact layout lines everywhere. These lines should be made with a marking gauge—or even better, with a mortise gauge that has two scribe points that can be set. This will give you the level of precision you'll need for accurate work.

When you're cutting with a router, the router bit usually defines the size of the mortise. And jigs, fences, stops, or guides determine both the size and the location of the cut, not multiple layout lines. Layout lines are necessary, but only to set up the jigs for the very first cut. Beyond this, layout is wasted effort. I usually make a simple mark to remind me where to cut the joint on a particular part. This is enough to get the part into the jig correctly. And if the jig is well made, repeatable accuracy should be a piece of cake.

4. Round over the ends of the tenons, and fit them into their mortises. Don't bother to round the lower sides of the upper rail tenons. You'll cut a dado through them in a later step.

Making mortises for the slats in the rails

Contemplating the 66 slats for the queen-size bed may be a little overwhelming, but they're really not that difficult or time-consuming to make because you don't have to cut mortises for all of them (unless you want to). The trick is to build what I call "constructed mortises." These mortises aren't cut out of solid stock but are assembled by inserting a dentil strip into a dado (see "Constructed Slat Mortises").

1. Cut a ½-in.-deep by ½-in.-wide dado centered on the top edge of the lower rails and the bottom edge of the top rails. Use a dado blade on the table saw to do this.
2. It's best to cut the notches for all four dentil strips in one board, then rip the individual strips out of this board. If you can't do this, you'll have to cut more notches. Start with a piece of wood ⁹⁄₁₆ in. by 2½ in. by 59⅜ in. long that is a reasonable color match for the rails.
3. Lay out the notch locations on one edge of this board.

Constructed Slat Mortises

Cutting each of these mortises individually would be tremendously difficult. Inserting a dadoed dentil strip into the upper and lower rails makes the joinery easy.

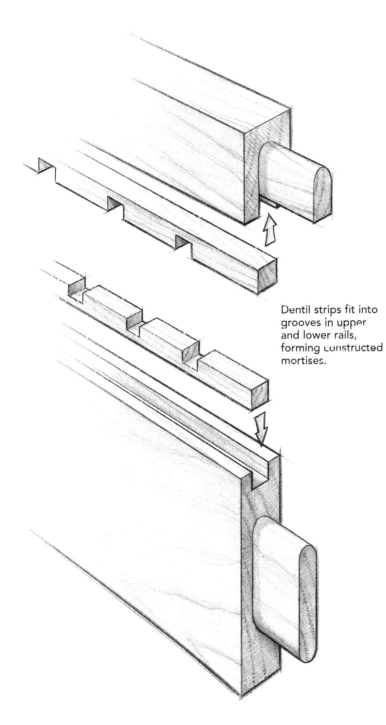

Dentil strips fit into grooves in upper and lower rails, forming constructed mortises.

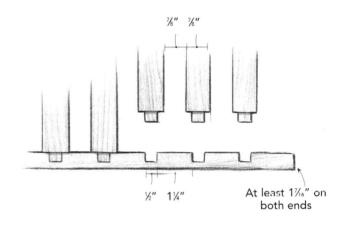

NOTCH LAYOUT FOR DENTIL STRIP

⅞" ⅞"

½" 1¼"

At least 1⁷⁄₁₆" on both ends

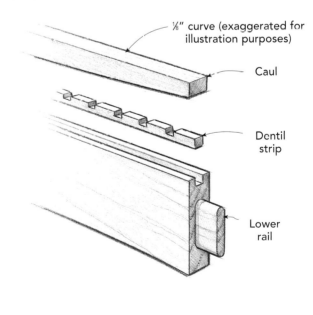

GLUING IN THE DENTIL STRIP

Use a slightly curved caul to distribute the clamping pressure.

⅛" curve (exaggerated for illustration purposes)

Caul

Dentil strip

Lower rail

Photo A: To cut all of the notches in the dentil strips for the constructed mortises, use a crosscut sled.

Tip: Mark both sides of each joint with a distinguishing letter or number so you don't get them mixed up later.

4. Cut the ½-in.-wide by ⁷⁄₁₆-in.-deep notches on the table saw with a ½-in.-wide dado cutter (see **photo A**). I cut the notches using a shop-built crosscut sled. It supports the strip well on both sides of the blade.

5. Make a reference mark across one end of the notched board. This will help you keep track of which way they go—and eliminate any problems if the notches are not perfectly symmetrical. Then rip each strip just slightly wider than the grooves (see **photo B**). Try to plan your rips so you get rid of any tearout from cutting the notches.

6. Carefully plane or sand the strips to fit the grooves in the rails. You'll have to support the fragile strips on both sides and take very light cuts to keep them from breaking as you plane (see **photo C**). You want the strip tight, but you should still be able to insert it into the groove with hand pressure.

Gluing the dentil strips in the rail grooves

1. Make some ¾-in. by 3-in. by 60-in. cauls to press the strips evenly and firmly into the grooves.

2. Plane a slight bow into the edge of the caul so that the ends are slightly narrower than the center (see "Constructed Slat Mortises" on p. 97). This helps apply pressure evenly without using every clamp in the shop.

3. Apply the glue sparingly and only to the bottom of the groove.

4. Line up the ends of the strip so that they are flush with the tenon shoulders on both ends of the rail, and press the strip down into the groove (see **photo D**).

5. Place the caul curved-side down on top of the strip, and clamp into place using as many clamps as needed to seat the strip.

6. Once the glue has dried, plane or sand off any protruding dentils flush with the rest of the rail. Be careful to keep the top of the rail flat, so the slat tenon shoulders will fit tightly.

Tip: If you spread the glue on the walls of the rail groove, you risk getting glue into the dentil strip mortises, which is a pain to clean out (remember there are 132 of them).

Photo B: Use a push stick to guide the thin and fragile strips past the blade, and use an outfeed roller (not shown in photo) if you don't have a helper.

Photo C: The notched strip is too flexible to plane without support. Two plywood strips clamped to the bench keep the strip from bending or breaking.

Cutting the curve on the bottom of the headboard and footboard rails

1. Spring a ⅜-in.- or ½-in.-thick by 1-in. scrap strip between the tenon shoulders to lay out the curve. Adjust the strip so that it just touches the bottom edge of the rail at both ends and is 1 in. up from the bottom edge at the center of the rail.

2. Cut the curve on a bandsaw or with a saber saw. In either case, stay to the outside of the line, and be careful cutting near the ends.

3. Smooth the curve with a flat-soled hand-plane skewed 45 degrees in the cut. This is fast and works well on gentle inside curves such as these (see **photo E** on p. 100). A belt sander and hand sanding using a curved block also do a good job.

Photo D: Slowly and carefully push the fragile dentil strip into the rail groove.

Making the slats

1. Calculate how many of each slat length you'll need based on the size of the bed. You'll get a slat for each 1 in. of width of board (assuming a ⅛-in. kerf). It's important to include enough wood for five or six extra slats; you'll want them to replace ones that warp or have loose tenons.

2. Rip the slats from ⅞-in.-thick flatsawn boards that have been handplaned and scraped or sanded on both faces first. This saves smoothing these two faces on the individual slats, which would be much more time-consuming. Rejoint the edge whenever you find that the wood is no longer straight enough.

3. To figure the exact lengths for the slats, dry-assemble the headboard and footboard frames. Measure the distance between the upper and lower rails, then add the tenon lengths. This should be ¹¹⁄₁₆ in. (¹¹⁄₃₂ in. for each of the two tenons).

4. Cut all of the slats for the headboard or footboard to exactly the same length on the table saw. Square up one end on each slat, then cut to length with the squared-up end against a stop.

Tenoning the slats

The slat tenons are easy to cut on the table saw, especially with a ⁵⁄₁₆-in.-wide dado cutter.

1. Make a wooden auxiliary fence for your table-saw miter guide or crosscut sled that extends 4 in. to 5 in. across the blade, and screw it into place.

2. Make a stop block for controlling the length of the tenon on the auxiliary fence. It's important that the face of the block be absolutely square, so check this carefully.

3. Clamp the stop block to the auxiliary fence on the far side of the blade, exactly the length of the tenon away from that side of the blade

TABLE-SAW SETUP TO TENON THE SLATS

The tenon is shaped by cutting on all four sides of the slat. This setup works on both a miter guide (shown here) and on a crosscut sled (shown in photo F).

Miter guide

Auxiliary fence

Stop block clamped to miter guide

Slat

Table saw

Dado blade, ⁵⁄₁₆" wide

(see "Table-Saw Setup to Tenon the Slats" and photo F).

4. Cut a slightly oversize test tenon on a cut-off piece of slat stock.

5. Check the fit of the test tenon in one of the mortises. Adjust the blade height if necessary so that you'll wind up with a snug-fitting tenon. Take your time to get it right. You don't want to have to trim too many of these tenons individually.

6. Cut shoulders on all four sides of each slat end.

Making the caps and drilling for attachment

These boards will be glued and screwed to the upper rails from underneath after the glue-up.

1. Mill the cap boards to size.

2. Lay out and drill six countersunk pilot holes in the upper rails centered between slat locations. Drill from the underside and angle the holes about 5 or 6 degrees toward the out-

Photo F: For cutting the tenons on the slats, the crosscut sled works well, though a miter gauge will work, too. The stop clamped on the far side of the sawblade registers the slat so the shoulder on each side of every slat will be cut the same.

Photo G: An angled
cradle helps drill the
angled pilot holes in
the upper rail for
the screws to attach
the cap.

*Tip: If you cut all of
the wings out of
rectangular boards,
2½ in. wide, the
waste piece can
function as a caul
when gluing the
wings to the legs.*

side of the bed. This will leave room for you
to drive the screws without too much interfer-
ence from the slats.

3. To drill the angled holes, use a strip of wood
rabbeted on an angle to hold the upper rails
in position on the drill press (see **photo G**).

Making the wings

The wings are both a decorative and a structural feature. They add another set of curved
lines to the bed and give depth to the headboard and footboard. They also support the
cap, making it sturdier.

1. Make patterns for the headboard and footboard wings on ¼-in. plywood or any compa-
rable thin material. Just enlarge the drawings
of the wings on p. 93.

2. Trace the pattern onto a piece of stock with
some consideration to the grain. It should
match the grain on the legs as well as possible
so that the wing looks like an integral part of
the leg and not an afterthought.

3. Smooth out the curves with planes, spokeshaves, scrapers, and/or sandpaper. The
four wings don't have to match precisely
because they'll never be seen right next to one
another.

ASSEMBLING THE HEADBOARD AND FOOTBOARD

Smoothing and checking the parts before assembly

Even with all of the parts cut and the joints fit, there's just a little more preparation necessary before you begin the glue-up.

1. Smooth all of the parts. If you presanded the slat stock before ripping, this is where you reap the benefits. There's still a lot of work to sand the other two faces on each slat, but it's half the time it would have been.

2. Ease all of the edges, either with a few swipes of a handplane, or by sanding with 220-grit sandpaper.

3. Check to be sure that each of the slats fits into the appropriate mortise in the lower and upper rails. It's worth checking every one. Trying to trim 33 of them during the glue-up with time running out could be a harrowing experience.

Assembling the slats and rails

Glue up the bed in stages. It does not work well to try to glue up everything all at once. Start with the headboard.

Photo H: Work quickly to get all of the slats in place before the glue sets. Organization is important here— a big hammer shouldn't be.

Tip: Don't try scraping around mortises when smoothing parts. The scraper will cut a noticeable dip on either side of a mortise. Careful sanding with a block that is no wider than the mortised part works best.

Photo I: Work on one tenon at a time. A clamp across one end lets you work across to the other side without any tenons coming loose.

Tip: Put all of the parts of the footboard to one side when you glue up the headboard so that you don't confuse them in the glue-up rush.

1. Get together all of the clamps, clamp pads or cauls, glue, glue spreaders, and the appropriate parts you'll need in one convenient place.

2. The slats and the rails go together first. There are a lot of parts to glue and get together, and not all that much time to do it in. Work steadily and methodically, but try to avoid frenzy. It also helps to use a slow-setting glue.

3. Smear a little glue into each of the mortises in a lower rail. Then insert the slats one at a time, until they are all in place. Try to get each slat to seat all the way. A tap or two with a non-marring mallet should help persuade those slats that don't want to go in easily (see **photo H** on p. 103).

4. Once all of the slats are set, spread glue into each of the upper rail mortises. Check

the orientation of this rail to be sure the appropriate tenon will line up with its corresponding mortise in the leg.

5. Insert the first slat tenon into the first mortise on the rail. You'll have to hold up the other end of the rail a little. The goal is to work on getting one slat into place at a time.

6. Place a clamp loosely across the end where some of the tenons have started in. This way these slats won't start popping out as you try to work farther along (see **photo I**).

7. Work steadily across to the other side, then tighten slowly and evenly. You'll have to add a few clamps to get even pressure all the way across the rails. You may want to shift some of the clamps around to clamp any open slat joints tighter.

8. Once everything is tight, check to be sure the assembly is reasonably square by measur-

A Flush-Cutting Jig

HOW THE JIG WORKS

Set the router bit depth to cut the thickness of the jig. Clamp the jig to the rail with the proud leg top protruding into the hole, and rout the leg flush.

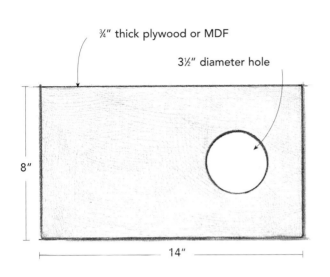

¾" thick plywood or MDF

3½" diameter hole

8"

14"

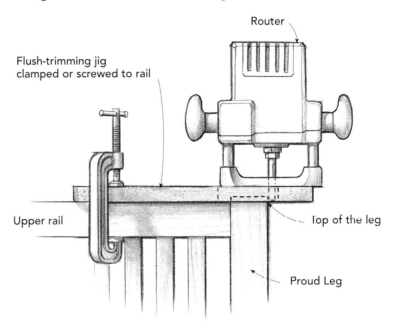

Router

Flush-trimming jig clamped or screwed to rail

Upper rail

Top of the leg

Proud Leg

---

ing the two diagonals. Adjust if necessary by loosening, then retightening the clamps at a slight angle in the direction of the long diagonal.

9. Let the assembly sit until the glue is cured.

Adding the legs

The legs go on after the rail and slat assemblies have dried.

1. Check to see if the rail tenons actually line up with the mortises. You can easily correct for minor misalignment by paring or rasping a little bit off the appropriate shoulder of the tenon.

2. Spread glue in the mortises and very lightly on the tenons, put the legs onto the rail assembly, and clamp tight.

3. Check again for square and adjust if necessary.

Cutting the legs and upper rails flush

For the cap to fit well, the rail and legs must be almost perfectly flush.

1. If the rail is slightly higher than the leg, it's easy to handplane away the difference. Be careful not to plane across the leg, or you might split a chunk of wood off on the outside.

2. If the leg is higher than the rail, the quickest way to trim it down is to rout it off. Use the jig described in "A Flush-Cutting Jig."

3. Clamp or screw the jig to the upper rail so the leg is roughly centered in the hole.

4. Set the depth of cut on the router so the bit just barely touches the top of the rail.

5. If you use a plunge router, raise up the bit to start the machine, then plunge down to the set depth.

Photo J: With the cap clamped into position, screw it into place. The scrap of wood I'm holding against the slats is important to prevent the drill chuck from marring the slats.

6. Rout clockwise slowly around the top of the leg to score the wood, then work your way in toward the center to complete the trim.

Adding the caps

1. Place the cap in position on the upper rail so it overhangs the legs by ⅛ in. toward the inside of the bed and overhangs the sides equally.

2. Mark its location by lightly tracing the top of the leg on the underside with a sharp pencil.

3. Remove the cap, spread a very thin film of glue on the top of the rail, and clamp the cap back in place without marring it.

Tip: If you use a regular router to trim the leg tops, install a guide bushing so you can keep the router bit away from the jig and leg when you start.

4. When you're sure the location is correct, drive in the screws from the underside of the rail using a long drill-mounted screwdriver bit. Slip a thin piece of wood between the drill chuck and the spindles to avoid marring the slats with the spinning chuck (see **photo J**).

5. Plug the pilot holes, and carefully cut them flush with a chisel.

Adding the leg hardware

As usual, I chose bed bolts for attaching the side rails to the headboard and the footboard. For visual reasons, the wings look much better if they end even with the bottoms of the rails. However, wings that low get in the way of a typical bed bolt hole. You can use this to your advantage: They make it possible to create a hidden joint. Just embed a nut in the outside of the leg and hide it with the wing. The bed bolts can be inserted from the inside of the rails using a special recess.

1. Mark both the outside and the inside of each leg 9 in. up from the bottom. (This should line up with the center of the rail.)
2. Measure from side to side on the leg to find the center, and mark with an awl.
3. Drill a ⅜-in. hole about halfway through from both sides of the leg. This will help keep the holes centered on both sides (it really needs to be on center on both sides of the leg).
4. When the holes meet up in the middle of the leg, drill through to clean up any misalignment.
5. Drill the two 5/16-in. alignment pin holes ⅜ in. deep on the inside of the leg. See "A Bolt Hole Drilling Guide" on p. 28 for a simple jig that helps with this. These holes should be 1½ in., center to center, both above and below the bolt hole and centered on the leg.

Embedding the square nuts in the legs
1. Use a nut to mark out the shape of the recess, first centering it over the ⅜-in. hole.
2. Chop with a chisel across the grain first, then with the grain, cutting down about 1/32 in. at a time until you reach the full depth needed to recess the nut just below the surface (see **photo K**).

Adding the wings
1. Hold each wing in place, centered on the leg to check that the top of the wing and the underside of the cap fit together well. Adjust the angle on top of the wing if necessary.
2. Hold each wing roughly in place again, but off to one side so you can mark the location of the bolt hole on the back of the wing.
3. Drill a shallow ½-in. recess in the back of the wing for room in case a bolt comes all the

Photo K: Chisel the recess for the nut around the ⅜-in. bolt hole on the outside of the leg. Chop across the grain first.

Photo M: Using the cutoff from bandsawing the wing as a caul makes it easy to clamp the wing in place and ensures even pressure.

Photo L: A recess in the back of the wing allows room for the bolt to come through the leg. Without it, the bolt will break the wing right off when you tighten it during assembly.

way through the leg and nut (see **photo L**). Use the wing cutoff (the caul) to hold the wing in position for drilling.

4. Insert the nuts into the recesses in the legs.

5. Spread glue lightly on the flat side of the wing, staying away from the edges to minimize squeeze-out.

6. Center each wing in place. It should be $7/16$ in. from either edge all the way down.

7. Place the caul over the wing, put a scrap strip of wood on the opposite face of the leg as a clamp pad, and clamp the wing into place using at least four or five clamps (see **photo M**).

MAKING THE SIDE RAILS

Sizing the side rails
The side rails are refreshingly simple after the complicated headboard and footboard.

1. Mill the rail stock to 1⅛ in. thick if you haven't done so already, and rip the rails to 6 in. wide.

2. To figure the length when using a box spring, add about ¼ in. to the length of the box spring. If you're using slats, leave more room—usually between ½ in. and 1 in. over the mattress length.

3. Cut the rails to length.

Cutting the joinery in the side rail ends
The end rails have alignment dowels, like the First Bed. For the reversed bed bolt, you need to cut a T-shaped recess on the inside face of the rail. The T-slot has space to insert the bolt into the hole in the long part of the T and room to tighten the bolt with a wrench at the top of the T (see "Side Rail and Leg Joinery Details").

1. Make a routing template to cut the T-shaped slot (see "T-Slot Routing Template" on p. 110).

2. Align the jig at the end of the rails on the inside face.

3. Cut the T-slots with a plunge router fitted with a ⅝-in. guide bushing and ½-in. straight bit (see **photo** N on p. 110).

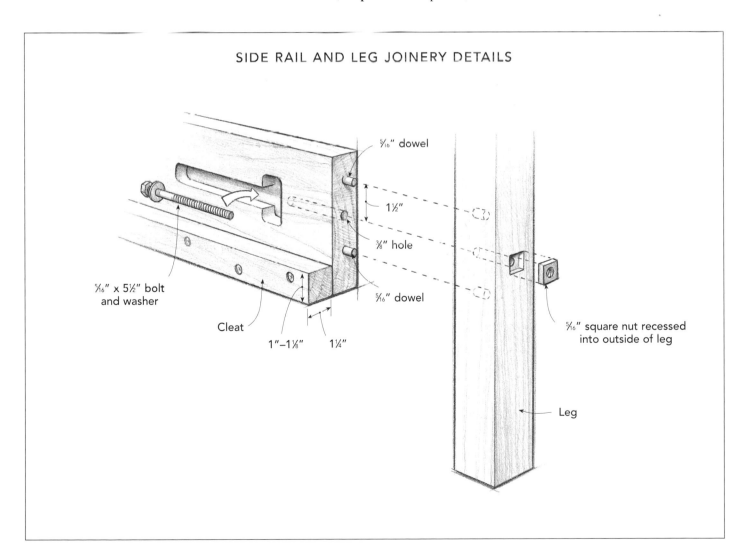

SIDE RAIL AND LEG JOINERY DETAILS

⁵⁄₁₆" dowel

1½"

⅜" hole

⁵⁄₁₆" dowel

⁵⁄₁₆" x 5½" bolt and washer

Cleat

1"–1⅛"   1¼"

⁵⁄₁₆" square nut recessed into outside of leg

Leg

Photo N: Rout the T-slot with a plywood jig as a guide. A cleat at the end of the jig aligns it on the rail.

Tip: It's important to apply the finish to the bed at a comfortable height. Place the parts on a low table or a pair of low sawhorses so you won't have to bend over so much to reach all of the slats.

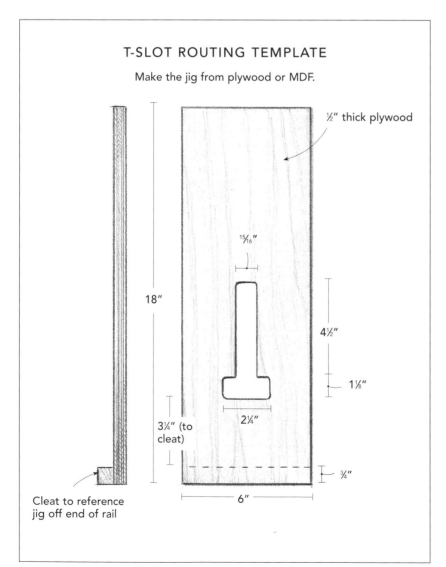

T-SLOT ROUTING TEMPLATE

Make the jig from plywood or MDF.

½" thick plywood

18"

$^{15}/_{16}$"

4½"

1⅛"

2¼"

3¼" (to cleat)

¾"

6"

Cleat to reference jig off end of rail

4. Drill the bolt and alignment holes in the ends of the rails using the jig described in "A Bolt Hole Drilling Guide" on p. 28.

5. Squeeze a little glue into the alignment pin holes, and insert the $^5/_{16}$-in. by 1¼-in. dowels.

Adding cleats or slats

1. Mill up two cleats 1 in. to 1⅛ in. thick, 1¼ in. wide, and ¹⁄₁₆ in. less than the length of the side rails. You can use some of the rippings from milling up the bed rails for this purpose, but any strong hardwood will work. You can also use any of the metal mattress hangers discussed on p. 89.

2. On the wider face of each cleat, drill a series of countersunk pilot holes for screws roughly 6 in. apart. I usually lay out these holes in a zigzag pattern, a little closer to one edge and then to the other.

3. Screw the cleats in place.

4. Mill up slats if you want to make this bed to support a mattress alone. Refer to the First Bed on p. 31-35 for details about making notched slats and adding dowel pins to the cleats.

FINISHING UP

Choosing a finish

Whatever finish you choose, you're in for a bit of work with all the surfaces. Here are some simple strategies for wet-sanding an oil finish or rubbing out a film finish.

1. To finish the slats, work from one side of the bed, and sand the face and one edge, whichever is the most comfortable. If you're right-handed, it's usually the right face, and vice versa.

2. Work your way across the great expanse of slats, then go around to the other side (or flip the bed around), and do the same thing with the opposite faces and edges. This is a good way not to miss any.

3. Don't bother finishing the cleats.

Final assembly

There are only minor differences in assembly on this bed. Because the nut is captured, each bolt needs only one washer. Assembly requires the same basic approach, but you are tightening from the inside.

Insert the bolt, and then use a ½-in. open-end wrench to tighten it (see **photos O** and **P**). Remember to install one rail to the headboard and footboard before moving on to the second rail.

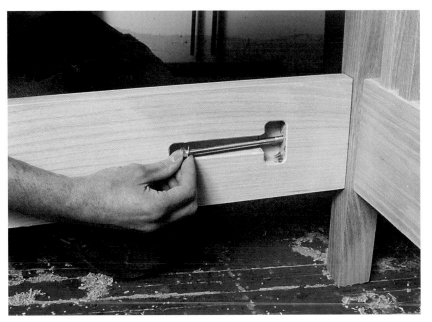

Photo O: To assemble the bed with T-slots, first insert the bolt and washer into the hole and push them forward.

Photo P: Then tighten the bolt with an open-end wrench. The space at the top of the T leaves room to rotate the wrench.

WINDSOR BED

The Windsor Bed is a design of simple good looks. It looks like a classic—something that has been around for ages. The visual relationship with Windsor chairs is obvious with the arches and spindles. But the history of this style of bed is younger, dating back to the early 1900s, when similar tubular metal beds were built (they're still made today in brass).

Part of the graceful nature of the headboard and the footboard comes from the way the arch and the legs are formed as a single bent element. But it's also important that each curve is half of an ellipse—the footboard a much flatter ellipse than the rounder headboard. An ellipse flows easily into the straight "leg" sections of the lamination in ways that simple curves would not. And the ellipses provide much more visual interest than a semicircle.

I've made more Windsor beds than any other type of bed—probably close to 200. It was one of my first designs and my first real success in woodworking. It was also the subject of my first woodworking article in *Fine Woodworking* magazine. And I still get a kick out of making them, although I now make a much wider range of pieces than I did 15 years ago. It's a refreshing change from custom designs to work on a piece where most of the problems have been worked out.

Windsor Bed

THE HEADBOARD AND FOOTBOARD LEGS are each a part of a single lamination bent into an elliptical arch. Dowels form the Windsor-like spindles between the rails and the bent member. Note that the headboard and footboard rails are through-tenoned and wedged into the laminated arches.

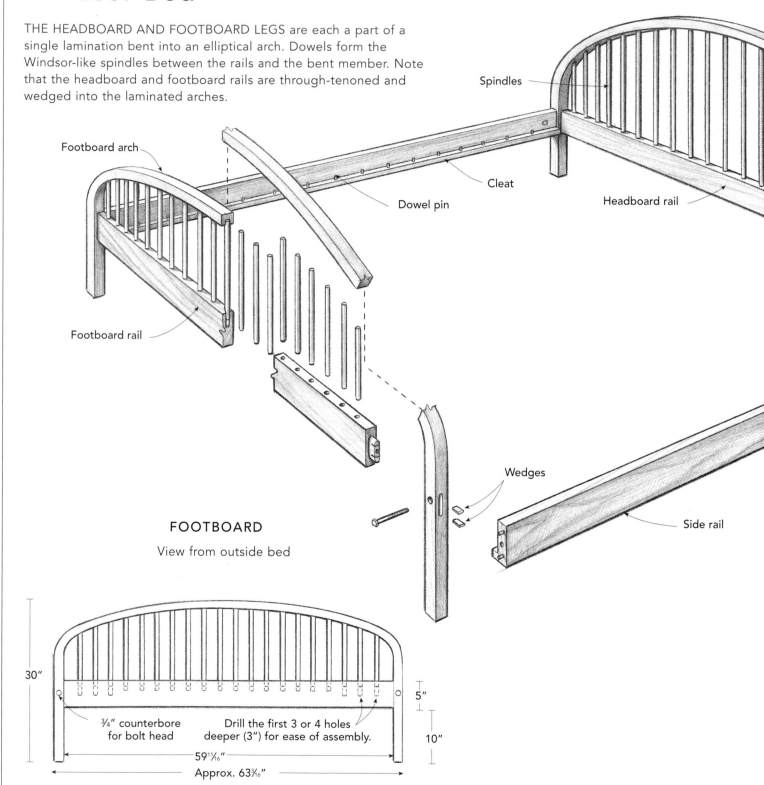

Footboard arch

Spindles

Dowel pin

Cleat

Headboard rail

Footboard rail

Wedges

Side rail

FOOTBOARD

View from outside bed

30"

5"

10"

¾" counterbore
for bolt head

Drill the first 3 or 4 holes
deeper (3") for ease of assembly.

59¹¹⁄₁₆"

Approx. 63³⁄₁₆"

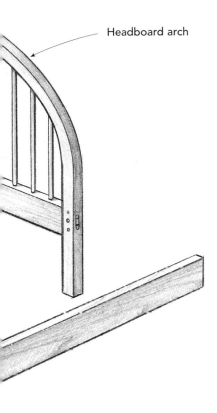

Headboard arch

CUT LIST FOR THE WINDSOR BED

Headboard and Footboard

34	Strips for lamination	$\frac{1}{10}$ in. x $2\frac{1}{4}$ in. x 120 in. (or 38 strips at $\frac{3}{32}$ in.)
2	Headboard and footboard rails	$1\frac{1}{16}$ in. x 5 in. x 64 in. (rough length)
40	Spindles	$\frac{5}{8}$ in. diameter x various lengths

Side Rails

2	Side rails	$1\frac{1}{16}$ in. x 5 in. x 81 in.
2	Cleats	1 in. x $1\frac{1}{4}$ in. x $80\frac{7}{8}$ in.
16	Slats	$\frac{3}{4}$ in. x 4 in. x $60\frac{1}{8}$ in.

Hardware

4	Hex-head bolts with nuts and washers	$\frac{5}{16}$ in. x $5\frac{1}{2}$ in.
8	Dowels (for alignment pins)	$\frac{5}{16}$ in. x $1\frac{1}{4}$ in.
32	Dowels (for slat pins)	$\frac{5}{16}$ in. x $1\frac{1}{4}$ in.

#6 x $1\frac{5}{8}$-in. screws, as needed

$\frac{5}{8}$-in. brads, as needed

These dimensions are for a queen-size bed. You may have to adjust your dimensions to suit the bed size, the mattress size, or any differences in wood dimensions.

HEADBOARD

View from inside bed

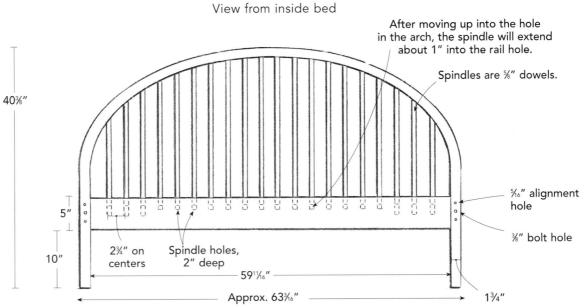

After moving up into the hole in the arch, the spindle will extend about 1" into the rail hole.

Spindles are $\frac{5}{8}$" dowels.

$\frac{5}{16}$" alignment hole

$\frac{3}{8}$" bolt hole

$40\frac{3}{8}$"

5"

10"

$2\frac{3}{4}$" on centers

Spindle holes, 2" deep

$59\frac{11}{16}$"

Approx. $63\frac{3}{16}$"

$1\frac{3}{4}$"

BUILDING THE BED STEP-BY-STEP

MAKING A WINDSOR BED means learning about bent strip lamination. Roughly a third of the project time goes into making the forms. The spindles take a trick or two to get into the headboard and footboard, but otherwise, the rest of the construction will be familiar territory from earlier chapters.

There are a few tools necessary to make a Windsor Bed. Figure a minimum of twelve 2-ft. bar clamps for gluing up the arches, plus two 6-ft. bar or pipe clamps—but more is always better with clamps. A jointer and a planer are almost essential for cleaning up the rough arches. It's possible to do it without them, but I'm not sure I'd have the fortitude to do it by hand.

BENDING THE HEADBOARD AND FOOTBOARD ARCHES

Building bending forms
The work begins with laying out and constructing the bending forms and cauls for the arches. There are two plywood forms, one for the headboard and one for the footboard. Each form needs a set of three curved cauls and two straight cauls to mold the lamination tightly and evenly to the form.

1. Build the ellipse layout jig, referring to "An Ellipse Layout Jig." If you don't want to build the jig, you can simply enlarge the drawings in "Bending Forms and Cauls" on p. 118.
2. To lay out the headboard arch form, set the adjustable blocks to half the minor and major diameters, 18⅝ in. and 29²⁷⁄₃₂ in. respectively. For the footboard, half the minor and major diameters are 8⅜ in. and 29²⁷⁄₃₂ in. respectively (see "Bending Forms and Cauls" on p. 118).
3. Scribe the ellipse directly on the ¾-in.-thick plywood you're using for the form (see **photo A**). You'll eventually need about four sheets of plywood to make the forms and cauls.
4. Cut out one D-shaped ellipse and its legs with a jigsaw, and sand the outside edge smooth and even.
5. Use this form to mark out the other two layers. Rough-cut each layer just to the outside of the line, screw and glue it to the smoothed form, and flush-trim with a router. Piece the middle layer together from off-cuts to save material.

Making the cauls
The cauls don't have the same shape as the form. Their curves have greater diameters because they conform to the outside of the arches. They're very simple to make though.

Photo A: To lay out the elliptical curves, screw the ellipse jig directly onto the plywood for the forms.

An Ellipse Layout Jig

This ellipse layout jig is scaled to draw bed-size ellipses.

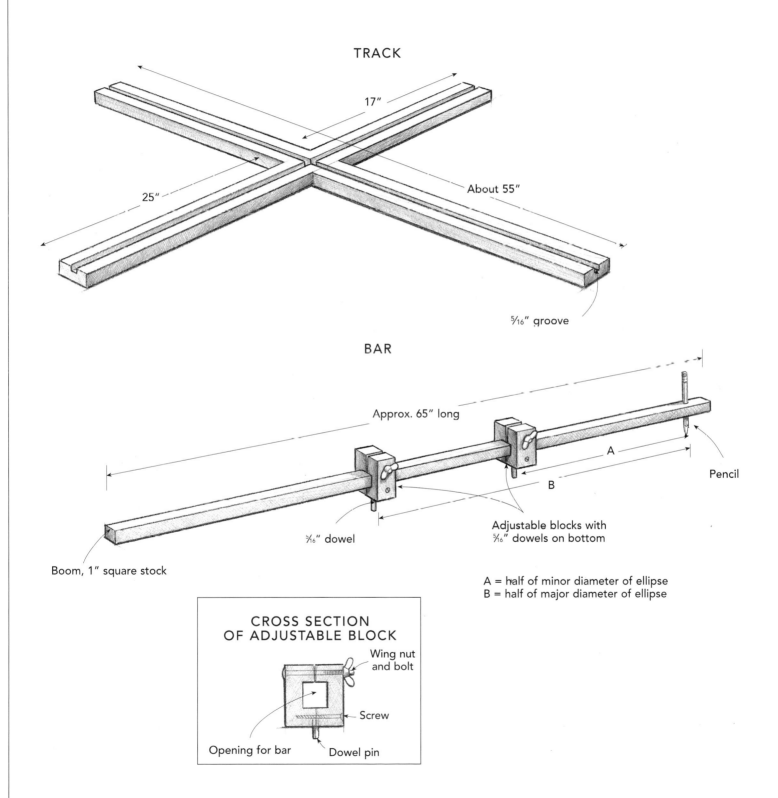

TRACK

17"

25"

About 55"

5/16" groove

BAR

Approx. 65" long

A

Pencil

B

5/16" dowel

Adjustable blocks with
5/16" dowels on bottom

Boom, 1" square stock

A = half of minor diameter of ellipse
B = half of major diameter of ellipse

CROSS SECTION
OF ADJUSTABLE BLOCK

Wing nut
and bolt

Screw

Opening for bar

Dowel pin

Bending Forms and Cauls

To mold the headboard and footboard arch, you need to make up forms and cauls for each.

FOR HEADBOARD

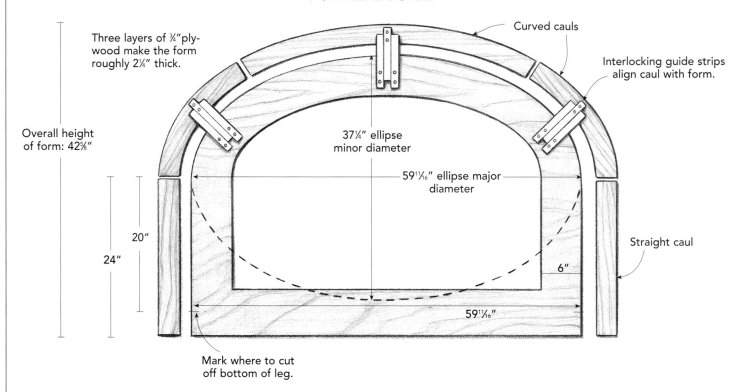

Three layers of ¾"ply-wood make the form roughly 2¼" thick.

Curved cauls

Interlocking guide strips align caul with form.

Overall height of form: 42⅝"

37¼" ellipse minor diameter

59¹¹⁄₁₆" ellipse major diameter

Straight caul

20"

24"

6"

59¹¹⁄₁₆"

Mark where to cut off bottom of leg.

FOR FOOTBOARD

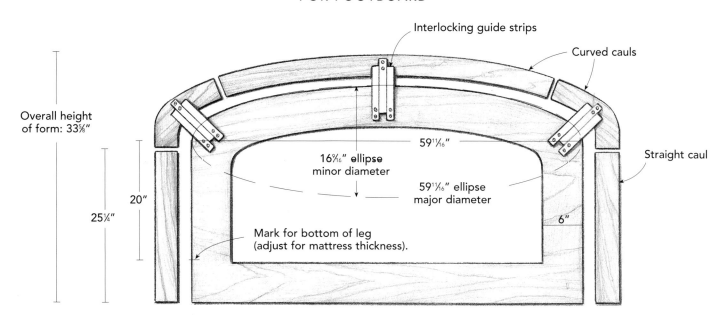

Interlocking guide strips

Curved cauls

Overall height of form: 33⅝"

59¹¹⁄₁₆"

16⅜₆" ellipse minor diameter

59¹¹⁄₁₆" ellipse major diameter

Straight caul

20"

25¼"

6"

Mark for bottom of leg (adjust for mattress thickness).

1. Make a 3½-in.-diameter disk of ¼-in. plywood, and drill a small hole in the center. Stick a pencil in the center hole and roll the disk around the outside of the forms to mark the curve of the cauls (see **photo B**).

2. After cutting and smoothing the three layers of plywood to shape, cut apart into three cauls.

3. Use two 2-in. by 2¼-in. by 24-in. boards—solid or glued up from the plywood scraps—to make the cauls for the straight sections.

4. Align the cauls on the form, and screw one guide strip on the cauls and two on the forms. These make it easy to align the cauls properly during the bend.

5. Wax the forms, cauls, and guide strips to keep the glue and lamination strips from sticking to them.

Cutting the strips for lamination

For the laminated curves, you need 34 strips, each roughly ¹⁄₁₀ in. thick, 2¼ in. wide, and 10 ft. long. There are two alternatives. These can be ripped from solid stock, or you can buy ¹⁄₁₀-in. veneer and cut it into 2¼ in. strips (see "Making vs. Buying Lamination Strips").

1. To mill your wood from solid stock, start with two 2¼-in.-thick boards each about 5 in. wide. This makes the wood easier and safer to handle and will reduce setup time during the actual rips.

2. Set up a featherboard to help hold the stock against the fence as you're ripping, and wax the rip fence to make the ripping easier.

3. Mark layout triangles on the faces of the boards so that you can put the strips back together in sequence.

Tip: If you don't have a good way to measure in tenths of an inch, you can make the strips ³⁄₃₂ in. thick, but you'll need 19 strips per lamination.

Photo B: Lay out the inside edge of the cauls 1¾ in. from the forms with a 3½-in. layout disk and pencil.

MAKING VS. BUYING LAMINATION STRIPS

I made my first Windsor Bed by gluing up strips ripped from solid stock. With an assistant, it took most of a day, with frequent breaks for the underpowered motor on my 8-in. saw to cool down, for resetting the tripped circuit breaker, and for sweeping up the dust. I swore off this method, found a source for veneer, and used it for the next 70 or so beds.

At first, I ripped the veneer with a circular saw and a long straightedge. Later, I moved on to cutting it on the table saw. Both methods work fine, but are fairly messy and awkward without a well-thought-out setup.

Veneer is expensive, especially when you take into account the large amount of scrap that is left over. You can use some of this waste in other lamination projects, but much of it is useless—unless you need a *lot* of ¹⁄₁₀-in. shims.

Ultimately I tried ripping from solid stock again using a more powerful saw, a better outfeed setup, and dust collection. I found that one person can easily do the whole job in a couple of hours. The results are noticeably better, too, with fewer gaps in the laminations and better finished surfaces. The deciding factor may be the saw you have and its (and your) tolerance for heavy ripping.

Photo C: There is a lot of surface area to cover with glue, so use a paint roller. The dried glue on the floor shows what happens if you don't use a tarp. I'd be more careful at home. (Photo by Strother Purdy, © The Taunton Press, Inc.)

MATTRESS THICKNESS AESTHETICS

As mattresses vary greatly in thickness, it's essential to measure the actual mattress to be used before you design your headboard and footboard. That way, you avoid making a headboard that ends up hidden by a very thick mattress.

Usually a matter of an inch or two is no big deal, but on the Windsor Bed the problem is more acute. You don't want the mattress to extend up over the curve of the footboard because it will look funny. With a thicker mattress, you will have to adjust the lengths of the straight portions of the arches. The measurements I've provided will work for a queen-size bed with a mattress 7 in. to 8 in. thick.

Tip: Do not try to rip those last couple of strips out of a board that is less than 1 in. thick. It's not worth the danger involved.

4. Set the fence on your saw so that a $\frac{1}{10}$-in. strip will be ripped off to the outside of the blade.

5. Rip both boards, then shift the fence over the thickness of the blade plus $\frac{1}{10}$ in. Joint the edges only when necessary. Try to keep the strips in sequence as they come off the board, referring to your layout triangles.

6. Cut all 34 strips 10 ft. long. You don't need the length for the footboard, but it simplifies the ripping (see "Mattress Thickness Aesthetics").

Gluing up the arches

Gluing up the laminated arches must be approached methodically. It won't hurt to do a dry run. Start with the headboard arch and do the footboard arch later in the same way.

1. Cover the floor with a large plastic tarp or two first, unless you don't mind getting glue all over it.

2. Spread out the bundle of strips on the tarp, setting one strip a little apart from the other 16 as a reminder not to spread glue on it.

3. Set the form on a tarp as well, a little away from the strips, or on a large enough worktable so that the form is fully supported, with cauls and clamps at hand.

Photo D: Start clamping the laminations at the center. Before aligning the cauls on the side, pull the ends around and hold them with clamps. This makes positioning the cauls much easier. (Photo by Strother Purdy, © The Taunton Press, Inc.)

Photo E: A wooden block between the clamp and the caul makes it possible to use a long clamp where a short one is needed. (Photo by Strother Purdy, © The Taunton Press, Inc.)

4. Prepare enough glue for a lamination (see "The Glue to Use" on p. 125).

5. Spread the glue evenly on one face of the 16 strips using a 9-in. paint roller with a short nap cover (see **photo C**).

6. Bundle the strips in order with the one unglued strip on top.

7. Lay the bundle at the top of the form and start clamping from the center.

8. Work alternately to the left and right, placing clamps both above and below the form.

9. After the first few clamps are on, pull the strips around each side, then hold them in place with a *loose* clamp (see **photo D**).

10. Working around the bends is most difficult because the clamps tend to get in the way of each other. Sometimes a block of wood can be used as a spacer between clamp and caul to help get the end of the clamp outside the clutter (see **photo E**).

11. Leave the laminations in the clamps overnight.

Finishing up the arches

1. Before you take the arches out of the forms, transfer the marks for the finished lengths of the legs onto them.

2. Once you unclamp and remove the arches, transfer these marks on the inside faces, where they won't get planed off. Crosscut the arches a few inches below these marks for now.

3. Joint an edge on the arches. Despite appearances, it really isn't a big deal to use a jointer for this (see **photo F** on p. 122). Keep as much of the arch as possible over the jointer table at all times. A wider jointer is also a big help here, but a 6-in. machine will do the job just fine with roller stands at both ends, or an assistant. Note: Cutting a lot of plastic resin glue is very rough on both jointer and planer knives.

4. Plane the legs to 1¾ in. thick. This is probably the strangest-looking procedure in the whole project: Simply steer the headboard or footboard arch through the planer, making sure it doesn't bind on the planer sides (see **photo G** on p. 122). Any planer wider than 10 in. should work fine.

5. Crosscut the arches to final length as marked.

6. Scrape and sand all faces of the arch, keeping the areas around the rail joints flat and square. A belt sander works well for everywhere but right around the joints.

Tip: An electric blanket (but not one you plan to use for sleeping after this) will help plastic resin glue cure if your shop will be cooler than 65°F.

Photo F: My wide jointer helps keep the lamination stable. But roller stands or an assistant can make jointing the arch on narrower machines possible.

Photo G: The curve in the arch doesn't affect the operation of the planer at all, though I look like I'm doing a hula dance.

ROUTER TEMPLATE FOR MORTISING THE LEGS

Guide strips center the jig on the lamination, and a stop block aligns it to cut the mortise 11⅛" from the bottom of the leg. Note that the opening in the template will be 11¹⁄₁₆" above the bottom of the leg. Use the template with a ½" router bit and a ⅝" guide bushing.

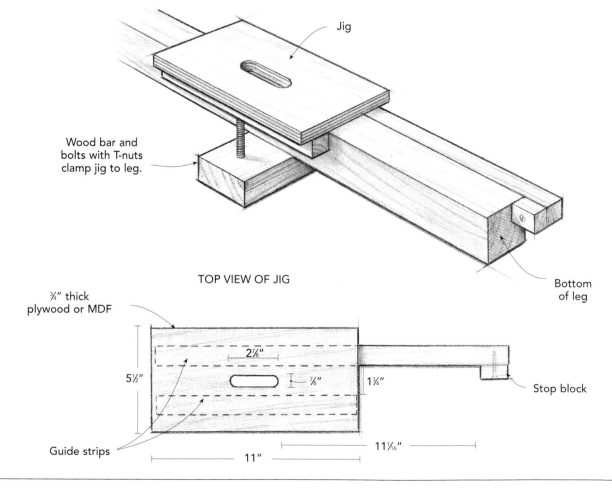

Jig

Wood bar and bolts with T-nuts clamp jig to leg.

Bottom of leg

TOP VIEW OF JIG

¾" thick plywood or MDF

2⅞"

5½"

⅞"

1¾"

Stop block

Guide strips

11"

11¹⁄₁₆"

Mortising the arches

A wedged mortise and tenon joins the rail to the arch. The mortises are located starting 11⅛ in. up from the bottom of the legs of the arches and are ¾ in. by 2¾ in.

1. Make a simple template for plunge-routing these mortises (see "Router Template for Mortising the Legs") and clamp it in place on the lamination.
2. Drill a few ⅜-in.-diameter holes straight through the lamination in the center of the mortise template to clear some of the waste and make the routing a little easier.
3. Plunge-rout in small increments. Clear away the dust to allow the guide bushing to trace the pattern accurately (see **photo H**).

MAKING THE HEADBOARD AND FOOTBOARD RAILS

Sizing the rails

1. Mill the rail stock to 1¹⁄₁₆ in. (or purchase 5/4 lumber surfaced to 1¹⁄₁₆ in.).
2. Joint one edge straight, then rip the rails to 5 in. wide.
3. Calculate the headboard and footboard rail length based on the actual thicknesses of the legs of the arches at the mortises.

Due to variations in the thickness of the strips compounded 17 times, the thickness can vary from side to side. I've had the two sides off by more than ¹⁄₁₆ in.

Use the formula from chapter 1 to arrive at the overall length, which for this bed runs like this:

$$L = 60\tfrac{1}{4} - \left(\frac{\text{leg thickness } 1 - 1\tfrac{1}{16}}{2}\right) - \left(\frac{\text{leg thickness } 2 - 1\tfrac{1}{16}}{2}\right) + \text{tenon}^1 + \text{tenon}^2$$

Tip: After calculating the rail length, add ¹⁄₃₂ in. to each of the rail tenons. This will make it easy to flush-cut them when assembled.

Template for Rounded Tenon Ends

TEMPLATE BLANK

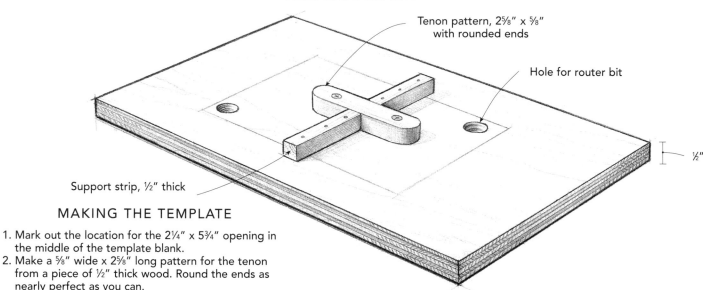

Tenon pattern, 2⅝" x ⅝" with rounded ends

Hole for router bit

Support strip, ½" thick

½"

MAKING THE TEMPLATE

1. Mark out the location for the 2¼" x 5¾" opening in the middle of the template blank.
2. Make a ⅝" wide x 2⅝" long pattern for the tenon from a piece of ½" thick wood. Round the ends as nearly perfect as you can.
3. Screw the pattern and two support strips to the template blank.
4. Drill two 1" diameter holes near diagonally opposite corners of the opening.
5. Set up a router table with a flush-trimming bit to run on the tenon pattern.
6. Place one of the holes in the template blank over the router bit so that it doesn't contact the bit. Hold the blank firmly, turn on the router, and rout the profile of the tenon and the opening.
7. Repeat this operation on the other side of the opening. Then remove the tenon pattern and support strips from the template.

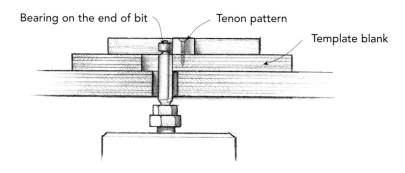

Bearing on the end of bit

Tenon pattern

Template blank

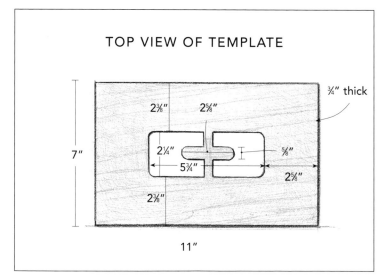

TOP VIEW OF TEMPLATE

¾" thick

7"

2⅜"

2⅝"

2¼"

5¾"

⅝"

2⅝"

2⅜"

11"

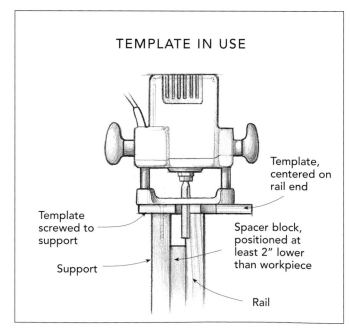

TEMPLATE IN USE

Template, centered on rail end

Template screwed to support

Spacer block, positioned at least 2" lower than workpiece

Support

Rail

THE GLUE TO USE

Not all glues are equal when it comes to bent laminations.

I use Weldwood-brand plastic resin glue. It doesn't creep under tension, which means that it doesn't slip from the constant pressure to straighten out that you have in a bent lamination. It also doesn't impart as much moisture to the wood as aliphatic resin glues do.

Plastic resin comes in a powder form that you mix with water. I find that 1,000cc of glue powder and 400cc of water are about right for one lamination. Because it's fairly difficult to get all of the lumps out of so much glue when stirring by hand, use a paint-mixing stirrer in an electric drill.

Plastic resin glue does need to be handled with much more care than most glues. Wear a mask to avoid breathing the powder, and wear gloves and goggles to prevent contact with the glue.

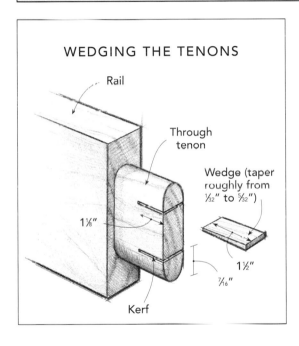

WEDGING THE TENONS

Photo I: This tenoning jig shapes the ends of the through tenons perfectly. It leaves an odd-looking strip on each cheek of the tenon, which is easy to trim off. (Don't let my aluminum jig intimidate you; it works fine if it's made of plywood.)

Cutting the tenons

Most tenoning jigs aren't set up to cut rounded ends. Since this bed has through tenons with rounded ends that show, I made up a router jig that cuts perfectly matching tenons quickly and easily (see "Template for Rounded Tenon Ends").

1. Rout the tenons so that they match their mortises perfectly (see **photo I**).
2. Chisel or plane off the two little "ears" that remain after routing.
3. Saw kerfs in the tenons for the wedges. Use a bandsaw with a fence or a handsaw (see "Wedging the Tenons").

Drilling for the spindles

1. Either mill or buy approximately 30 spindles, ⅝ in. by 36 in. long. I've found that making the spindles is an awful lot of work, and it's difficult to keep a consistent size. Now, I just buy them.
2. Mark out 20 centers for the spindle holes on the headboard and footboard rails 2¾ in. apart.
3. Dry-assemble the rails with the arches. First insert one tenon into its mortise most of the way, and then spring the arch open enough to slip the other tenon in.

are *very* difficult to install after the rail and arch are glued up.

7. Clamp the arches upside down in a bench vise, with the straight legs perpendicular to the bench surface. A support stick clamped to the far side of the arch and extending down to the floor will make it more stable.

8. Use a portable drill to cut the holes in the arches, aligning each by eye. To help drill straight, stand a square upright on the bench next to where you're drilling, and use it to align the drill (see **photo J**).

9. To drill on the steep angles at the ends of the arch, use a ⅝-in. Powerbore bit or any bit with a long pilot point. On the two outermost holes on the headboard arch, you may have to start the bit at an angle and then straighten up as you drill to keep it from drifting.

10. Gouge or rasp any holes on the ends that aren't perfectly straight to accommodate the spindles at the proper angle.

HEADBOARD AND FOOTBOARD ASSEMBLY

Preparation for assembly

My key discovery in developing this bed design was that the spindles can and should go in after the arches and rails are glued together. This works very well and takes a lot of the stress out of the glue-up.

1. Ease the edges of the arches with a ¼-in.-radius roundover bit. Chamfer the edges of the rails slightly.

2. In the footboard rail, determine the lengths of the three or four spindles on each end.

3. Place the rail against the bending roughly where it will be when installed. Don't bother to actually insert tenons into mortises, however. Just measure up from the bottom of the leg to the bottom of the rail on both sides to be sure the rail is in the right place.

Photo J: Sighting down the square helps you drill parallel to the sides of the lamination. First square up the sides of the arch to the bench.

4. With a large shopmade square, transfer the centerlines of the holes in the rail up onto the arches.

5. Square these marks around to the underside of the arch. To locate the spindle holes on center, draw a line with a marking gauge along the inside face of the arch.

6. Disassemble the headboard and footboard and drill ⅝-in. holes 2 in. deep in the rails with a drill press. Drill the three or four outer holes on each end of the footboard rail a full 1 in. deeper so you can insert those spindles before gluing the arches and the rails. They

Photo K: You'll use a bit of muscle to spring the rail into place. You could also spread the lamination with bench dogs and the tail vise of a suitably sized workbench.

4. Measure from the bottom of each of the six holes to about 1 in. below the arch and cut the spindle to length.

5. Insert these three or four spindles on each end before the glue-up begins. You must do this now because these spindles are too short to bend into place like the others. Then insert the spindles into the appropriate holes. Believe it or not, *don't use glue*. Leave the spindles in place during footboard glue-up.

Also, cut wedges for the tenons in a contrasting wood (I used maple here) and have them ready.

Gluing up

1. Spread glue in the mortises and very lightly on the rail tenons, slip one end in, and spring the bending open enough to slip the other end in. On the footboard, this does take some effort, and you may want to enlist some help (see **photo K**).

2. To clamp the tenons tight, use your two longest clamps (fitted with pads), and fit them above and below the joints from opposite sides of the frame. If you don't have clamps long enough, buy them before you start.

3. Spread glue on the wedges and hammer them in, tapping the wedges in evenly (alternating hammer blows).

Fitting the spindles

Installing the spindles after the glue-up makes the overall assembly much easier. You can work at your own pace because there is no pressure to get everything into place all at once. You can measure for the rest of the spindles while the clamps are still in place.

1. Measure from the bottom of each hole on the rail to just below the bending at the corresponding hole.

2. Cut dowels to length, and number them for location.

3. Check for fit in the test block, and sand or heat to fit if necessary (see "Cooking Spindles to Fit" on p. 128).

4. One at a time, insert the spindles into their holes in the rail (again, do not use glue). Flex the spindle a little while pushing down so that it seats all the way (see **photo L** on p. 128).

5. When bottomed out in the hole, the spindle should just fit inside the arch under its hole. If for some reason a spindle is too long, carefully trim it down in place with a handsaw.

6. Continue until all of the spindles are in place, leaving the spindles loose on top for the moment.

Tip: Listen for the tapping sound to change to a duller thudding to indicate when the wedges are in all the way.

COOKING SPINDLES TO FIT

It's important to be certain that the spindles will fit in their holes but be tight for years to come.

To ensure this, make up a test block drilled with the same drill bits (and to the same depths) you used for both the rail and the arch. Check the fit on both ends of every spindle, and sand to fit if necessary. Discard spindles that are too loose.

To speed this process, you should first shrink the ends of the spindles a little by inserting them in a can of hot sand an hour or two before assembly. The hot sand shrinks the wood by drying it. You'll be surprised how well it works. Be sure to keep the temperature of the sand no hotter than 170°F or you'll scorch the spindles. A meat thermometer will read the temperature easily.

After the bed is assembled, the spindles will grow back to size and lock themselves in place.

Photo L: Push with the lower hand to bow the spindle a little, so that the lower part aims straight into the hole. It's much easier to insert it into the hole this way.

Sand in a can on a hot plate will effectively shrink dowel ends, making it easier to insert them into their mortises.

7. Tap (or pound) the shorter spindles on the footboard in place if they don't go in by hand. Insert a piece of ¼-in. plywood between the spindle and the arch to protect the latter from damage when pounding.

8. When the glue for the rail joints is dry, remove the clamps from the arch.

9. Trim the wedges with a handsaw, and sand flush with the arches.

10. Clamp the assembled headboard or footboard upside down in your bench vise.

11. Spread a little glue around in each of the spindle holes in the arch, and push the spindles in all the way.

12. Remove the arch from the vise, and pin the bottoms of the spindles in place in the rails (not the arches) with ⅝-in. brads. Be sure to pin the inside face of the rail.

MAKING THE SIDE RAILS AND FINISHING UP

Milling the bed rails to length

Cut the side rails to length. Add about 1 in. to the mattress length to allow a little room for tucking in sheets and wiggling toes.

The queen-size bed should be 81 in. between headboard and footboard. For a bed with a box spring and mattress, the rails should be only 80¼ in. long (¼ in. longer than the actual box-spring length).

Installing the bed bolts

1. Drill a ⅜-in. hole centered on each end of both side rails, extending into the recess (see "Detail of End of Rail").
2. Drill two 5/16-in. holes 1 in. deep for the dowel pins using a doweling jig or the guide shown in "A Bolt Hole Drilling Guide" on p. 28.
3. Drill or rout the nut recesses ⅞ in. deep on the insides of the rails (see "A Template for Routing Nut Recesses" on p. 32).
4. Drill the ¾-in. counterbore ⅜ in. deep on the outside faces of the legs, centered and 12½ in. up from the bottom.
5. Drill a ⅜-in. hole in the center of the counterbore, all the way through the legs of the arch.
6. Drill holes in the leg to match the dowel alignment pins. They are 5/16-in.-diameter holes about ½ in. deep and 1½ in. above and below the ⅜-in. hole.
7. Squirt some glue into the holes in the ends of the rails, and insert 5/16-in. by 1¼-in. dowels.

Adding cleats, slats, and coats of finish

1. Apply the finish of your choice to the bed. Between coats, work on the cleats, and if this is to be a platform bed, the slats.

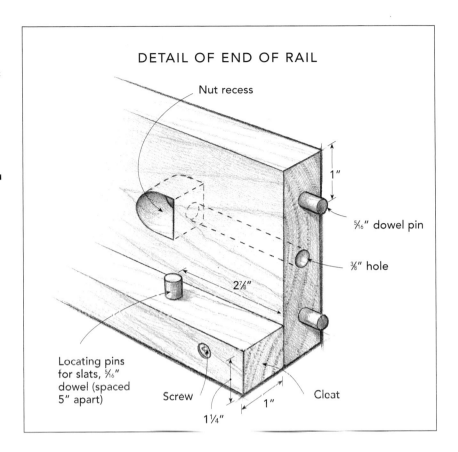

DETAIL OF END OF RAIL

Nut recess

1"

5/16" dowel pin

⅜" hole

2⅞"

Locating pins for slats, 5/16" dowel (spaced 5" apart)

Screw

1¼"

1"

Cleat

2. Mill the wood for the cleats, 1 in. by 1¼ in. by 80⅞ in.
3. Drill countersunk holes for screws on the cleats. They should be spaced roughly every 6 in. or 7 in. on one of the 1¼-in.-wide sides.
4. Drill 5/16-in. holes for slat-locating dowel pins about ¾ in. deep and spaced 5 in. apart on a narrower side of the cleat.
5. Put a little glue in the holes and pound in the slat pins, but don't attach the cleats to the rails until after finishing the rails.
6. Mill up 16 slats for a queen-size bed, ¾ in. by 4 in. by 61 in. in rough length, and chamfer the edges slightly.
7. Once the bed is together, measure the exact length for the slats, and cut them to size.
8. Notch the ends so they can slip onto the pins (see "A Jig for Notching Bed Slats" on p. 34).
9. Drop the slats into place, and step back to admire your handiwork.

Tip: For a bed with a box spring and mattress, make cleats for the headboard and footboard (but skip the slat pins).

PLATFORM BED

Say "platform bed" and this is the style of bed most people envision. It has become a very common way to put together a bed. In fact, the very first bed I made was a simple platform bed of this type. This was years before I considered myself a woodworker, and the results were pretty crude indeed. I screwed together some 2x12s for a base box and put an old cut-down Ping-Pong table on the top. That was it. No headboard, no side or footboard rails, no real support to keep the Ping-Pong table–style platform from sagging in the middle.

Fifteen years of professional furniture making and design have changed a lot of things, but I find that the simplicity of a "platform-on-a-box" type bed still works. Here, I've dressed it up a little, and in the process made it a bit more complicated to build. I've also worked to give the platform the appearance of floating to lighten up what can be a pretty heavy-looking piece of furniture. You could paint the base box black to make it disappear even more. But I like the look of the wood, and I like to treat it with a moderate dose of craftsmanship.

Notice that the more visible parts of the bed are not at all structural—they just rest on top of the platform.

Platform Bed

THE PLATFORM BED has three main parts. The first is the base box, made of plywood sides and solid wood corners joined with table leg brackets. The second is the headboard and rail assembly—the part you really see. It's built with solid wood rails, posts, and a headboard panel. The third is the platform itself, simply two plywood sheets joined with a hinge, which joins the base box and headboard assembly.

BASE BOX AND PLATFORM ASSEMBLIES

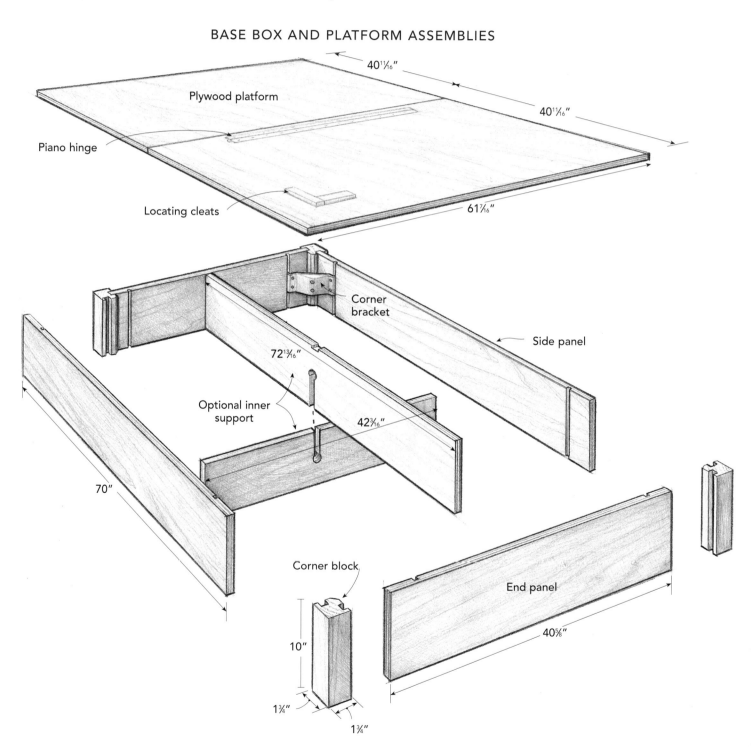

40 11/16"

Plywood platform

40 11/16"

Piano hinge

61 7/16"

Locating cleats

Corner bracket

Side panel

72 13/16"

Optional inner support

42 3/16"

70"

Corner block

10"

End panel

40 5/8"

1 3/4"

1 3/4"

HEADBOARD AND RAIL ASSEMBLY

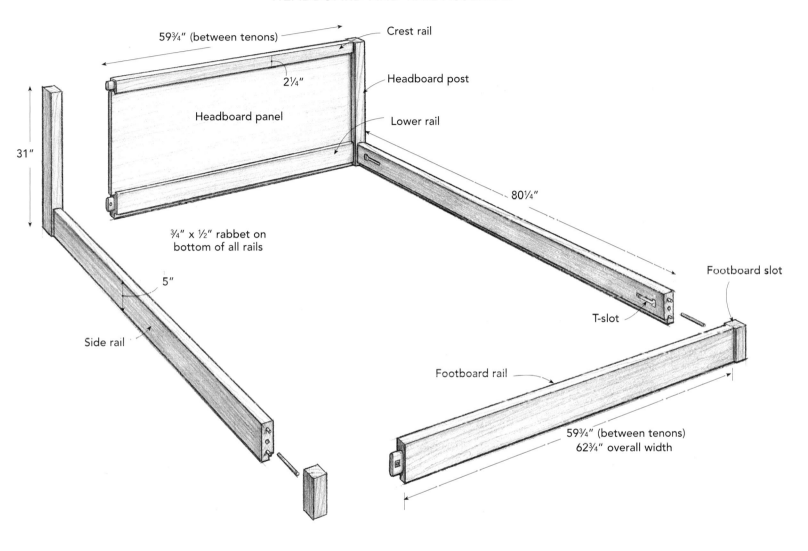

59¾" (between tenons)

Crest rail

2¼"

Headboard post

Headboard panel

Lower rail

31"

80¼"

¾" x ½" rabbet on
bottom of all rails

Footboard slot

5"

T-slot

Side rail

Footboard rail

59¾" (between tenons)
62¾" overall width

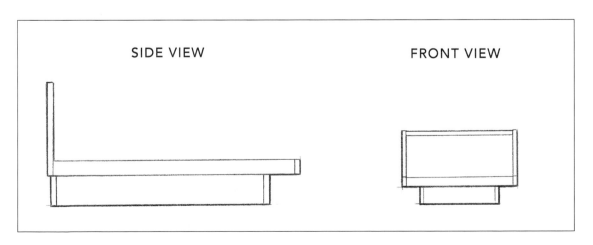

SIDE VIEW

FRONT VIEW

BUILDING THE BED STEP-BY-STEP

CUT LIST FOR THE PLATFORM BED

Base Box

4	Base box corners	1¾ in. x 1¾ in. x 10 in., solid cherry
2	Base box ends	¾ in. x 10 in. x 40⅝ in., cherry plywood
2	Box sides	¾ in. x 10 in. x 70 in., cherry plywood
1	Top-to-bottom inner support	¾ in. x 10 in. x 72¹³⁄₁₆ in., plywood
1	Side-to-side inner support	¾ in. x 10 in. x 42³⁄₁₆ in., plywood

Plywood Platform

2	Plywood platform halves	40¾ in. x 61¼ in.
8	Cleats	¾ in. x 1 in. x 6 in.

Headboard, Footboard, and Side Rails

2	Headboard posts	1¾ in. x 1¾ in. x 31 in.
2	Footboard blocks	1¾ in. x 1¾ in. x 5¹⁄₁₆ in.
1	Footboard rail	1¹⁄₁₆ in. x 5 in. x 62⁹⁄₁₆ in.
1	Headboard rail	1⁹⁄₁₆ in. x 5 in. x 62⁹⁄₁₆ in.
1	Crest rail	1⁹⁄₁₆ in. x 2¼ in. x 62⁹⁄₁₆ in.
2	Side rails	1¹⁄₁₆ in. x 5 in. x 80¼ in.
1	Headboard panel	¾ in. x 24⁹⁄₁₆ in. x 60½ in., plywood

Hardware

4	Traditional bed bolts	
4	Tabletop corner brackets	
1	Piano hinge	1½ in. x 48 in.
8	Dowels (for alignment pins)	⁵⁄₁₆ in. x 1¼ in.

#6 screws, as needed

These dimensions are for a queen-size bed. You may have to adjust your dimensions to suit the bed size, the mattress size, or any differences in wood dimensions.

THOUGH THIS BED stands on a base box instead of legs, the milling, cutting, and mortising of the headboard posts and the footboard blocks (not quite posts because they're only 5 in. long) proceed much as they have on many of the beds in this book. Begin work with the base box, then move to the plywood platform and finally the headboard and rail assembly, if only for the logic of building the bed from the ground up.

MAKING THE BASE BOX

Making the sides, ends, and corner blocks

1. Rip four 10-in.-wide strips out of a sheet of plywood for the box sides and ends.
2. Cut the plywood to length, 70 in. long for the side panels and 40⅝ in. long for the end panels.
3. Mill up a piece of solid wood 1¾ in. by 1¾ in. by about 4 ft. long for the corner blocks.
4. Rip dadoes, approximately ²³⁄₃₂ in. wide, on two adjacent sides of the blocks (see **photo A**). These dadoes will house the plywood panels. The plywood should fit snug but not so tight that you risk cracking off part of the solid wood.
5. Crosscut the corner blocks to exactly the same length as the width of the base box sides (10 in.).
6. For beds larger than queen size, make some kind of internal support inside the base box (see "Inner Support for Larger Bed Sizes").

Photo A: Cut the grooves for the plywood in the corner blocks with a dado blade before cutting the blocks to length. It's both easier and safer.

Tip: You should adjust the depth and exact location of your dadoes in the corner blocks so the overall size of the base box is 72½ in. by 43¾ in.

INNER SUPPORT FOR LARGER BED SIZES

If you're building this bed larger than queen size, you need to add an interior structure to support the platform. On the queen size, it's a toss-up whether or not to include one. Without a support, there will be a little bit of sag in the platform but maybe not enough to be a problem.

I make a simple inner support from two pieces of plywood (refer to "Platform Bed" on p. 132). It's a half-lapped X that stands inside the base box.

1. Rip two pieces of any plywood 10 in. wide.
2. Cut them to length so they just fit inside the assembled base box.
3. Find the centers of the two boards, and drill a 1½-in. hole through them.
4. Mark out and cut a half-lap joint in each board. This can be done with crosscuts on the table saw, stopping just as you get to the hole in the center.

Take multiple passes with a crosscut blade to cut the half-lap joint in the support structure. Don't just make a cut at either end of the notch because you'll get a trapped cutoff.

BASE BOX CORNER DETAIL

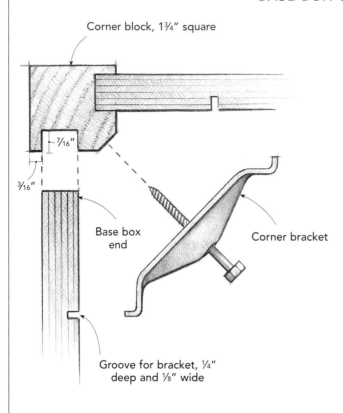

Corner block, 1¾" square

7/16"

3/16"

Base box end

Corner bracket

Groove for bracket, ¼" deep and ⅛" wide

The corner bracket provides an easy and secure way to join the base box together. These brackets are normally used to hold legs to aprons on tables—that's what the extra holes near the sides are for.

Assembling the base box

Use corner brackets designed for table aprons to connect the base box frame (see "Base Box Corner Detail"). These brackets allow the frame to be assembled quickly and solidly.

1. Cut a ¼-in.-deep by ⅛-in.-wide kerf across each end of the box sides (on the insides; see **photo B**). The location of this kerf depends on the corner bracket you use. Use your actual brackets to lay out the kerfs before you cut them.

2. Rip a ¼-in. chamfer on the inside corner of the corner blocks.

3. Drill two pilot holes on the drill press for bolting the corner bracket into the inside corner of each corner block. Support the blocks in a V-shaped groove jig (see **photo C**).

MAKING THE PLYWOOD PLATFORM

Cutting and connecting the plywood halves

The plywood platform should be just less than 1 in. longer and wider than the distance between the rails of the headboard assembly. On this queen-size bed, the upper frame is 60¼ in. by 80⁹/₁₆ in. between the rails. So cut two pieces of plywood to 61¼ in. by 40¾ in. Make the mattress platform in two halves if you're building anything bigger than a twin-size bed.

Photo B: When cutting the grooves in the sides and ends of the base box, align the cut against a stop block clamped to the fence.

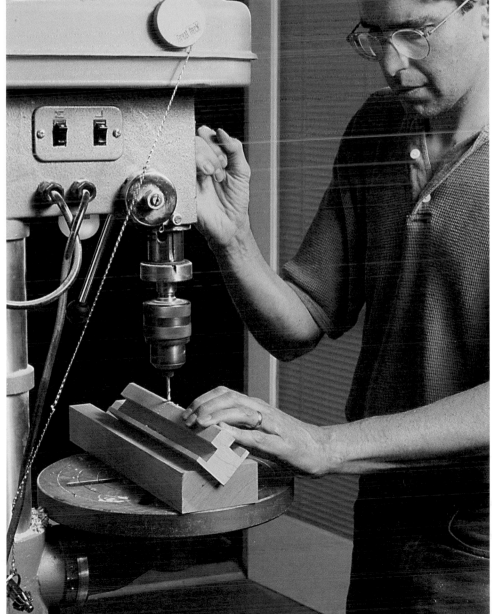

Photo C: A V-shaped groove jig helps you drill the holes for the screws in the corners of the base blocks.

Photo D: Screw the locating cleats to the platform against the edge of the base box. Don't snug them up too tight or it will be hard to drop the platform into place.

Tip: Instead of using a hinge to join the platform parts, you could cut biscuit slots in both halves, and glue the biscuits into the slots on just one side.

1. Cut the platform or platform parts to size.
2. If necessary, attach the two halves with a 1½-in. by 41-in. piano hinge. As piano hinges are generally sold in foot-long increments, just cut 7 in. off a 48-in.-long hinge.
3. Attach the hinge to the bottom faces so it doesn't snag on the mattress and tear it. The hinge will keep the halves aligned and together, allowing you to fold up the platform for moving.

Attaching the cleats and notching for the support

Cleats attached to the underside of the plywood will align the platform on the box.

1. Place the platform upside down on the floor, and assemble the support box on the platform.

2. Align the box so it's centered from side to side and flush with the edge of the plywood at the head. The solid wood corners should overhang the platform just a little.
3. Use the edge of the box structure to lay out the cleats on the inside.
4. Screw a pair of ¾-in. by about 1-in. by 6-in.-long blocks at each corner (see **photo D**).
5. Chamfer the blocks on the side away from the plywood to make it easier to drop the platform onto the box structure during assembly.
6. If you're using an inner support, mark where the piano hinge crosses the support and cut a notch (see **photo E** on p. 140).
7. Remove the inner support and cut out the notch.
8. Disassemble the box, and move the plywood platform to an out-of-the-way place.

MAKING THE HEADBOARD ASSEMBLY

Milling the headboard posts and footboard blocks

1. Mill stock for the posts and blocks to 1¾ in. square.

2. Cut the headboard posts to length, but leave the two footboard blocks as a single, longer board for now. They will be easier to mortise if you have a little more wood to hold onto.

3. Mark out and cut all the mortises (see "Mortise Details for Headboard Posts and Footboard Blocks").

4. Cut the footboard blocks to length. They should be ⅛ in. longer than the width of the rails.

Milling the rails

1. Mill the side rails and the footboard rail to 1¹⁄₁₆ in. thick.

2. Mill the lower and crest headboard rails to 1⁹⁄₁₆ in. thick. I find that a thinner upper rail feels springy when you lean against it, and the lower headboard rail should match the crest.

3. Rip the crest rail to 2¼ in. wide and all of the other rails to 5 in. wide.

4. Cut the rails to length, using the formula in "Determining Rail Lengths" on p. 11 if necessary.

5. Mark out the tenons. The distance between the tenons on all three of these rails should be 59¾ in.

6. Cut the tenons on the headboard and the footboard rails, and fit them to their mortises. The crest rail tenon should be located just above where you'll cut the dado for the headboard panel, so you can cut and fit it to the mortise as well.

Drilling and routing for the headboard bed bolts

Since the headboard will most likely be up against a wall, it doesn't matter if the holes show. So I use the simplest bed bolt method (also used in the First Bed on pp. 18-35).

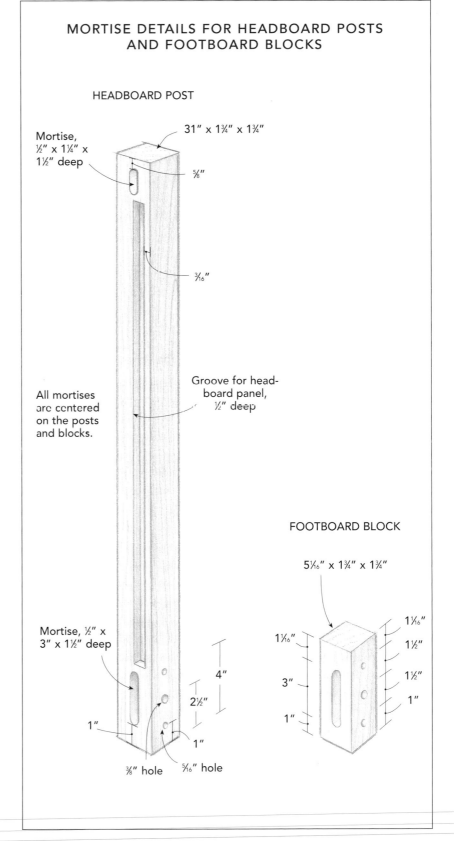

MORTISE DETAILS FOR HEADBOARD POSTS AND FOOTBOARD BLOCKS

HEADBOARD POST

31" x 1¾" x 1¾"

Mortise, ½" x 1¼" x 1½" deep

⅝"

³⁄₁₆"

All mortises are centered on the posts and blocks.

Groove for headboard panel, ½" deep

Mortise, ½" x 3" x 1½" deep

4"

2½"

1"

1"

⅜" hole   ⁵⁄₁₆" hole

FOOTBOARD BLOCK

5¹⁄₁₆" x 1¾" x 1¾"

1¹⁄₁₆"   1¹⁄₁₆"

1½"

3"   1½"

1"   1"

Photo E: Notch the head-to-foot plank of the support structure for the hinge. The hinge isn't centered on the support because the platform extends over the footboard side of the bed.

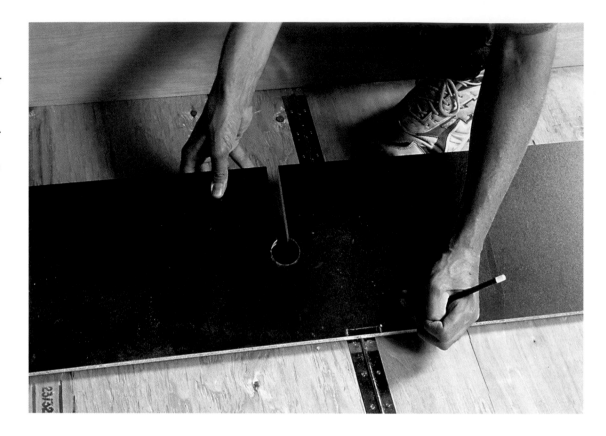

1. Counterbore the outside of the headboard post.
2. Drill the ³/₈-in. bolt hole and the two ⁵/₁₆-in. holes for the alignment dowels.
3. Drill both ends of the side rails for the bolt and alignment dowels.
4. Rout the D-shaped recesses for the nuts on the headboard ends of the rails.

Drilling and routing for the footboard bed bolts

Though it doesn't matter for the headboard, bolt holes would show in the footboard blocks. So I hide the nut in the footboard block (see "Embedding the Bed Bolt Nut in the Footboard Rail Tenon").

Tip: Set the depth stop on the router carefully. You want to rout just deep enough to leave ⅛ in. of wood between the bottom of the recess and the outside face of the rail.

1. Mark for the two ⁵/₁₆-in. alignment and ³/₈-in. bolt holes on the footboard block—only on the side rail side.
2. Drill the two ⁵/₁₆-in. holes, about ½ in. deep.
3. Drill the ³/₈-in. center hole. Do not drill all the way through the block; stop about ¼ in. shy of the outside face.
4. Rout T-shaped recesses for the bolts on the side rail ends. To do this, you'll need a plunge router outfitted with a ⅝-in. guide bushing, a ½-in. bit, and the router template described for the Craftsman-Style Bed (see p. 110).
5. Drill the bolt and alignment holes in the side rail.
6. Dry-assemble the footboard rail with the two footboard blocks and clamp them tightly.
7. Redrill through the center ³/₈-in. hole on each block so that each footboard rail tenon now has a hole. Don't drill all the way through.
8. Unclamp and remove the blocks from the rail.
9. Embed a ⁵/₁₆-in. square nut in the outer side of the tenons. To help you locate the nut properly, thread a ⁵/₁₆-in. bolt through the hole

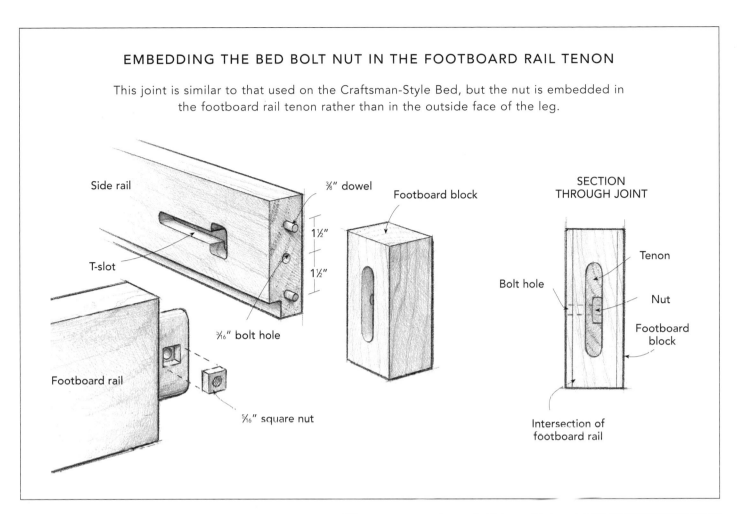

EMBEDDING THE BED BOLT NUT IN THE FOOTBOARD RAIL TENON

This joint is similar to that used on the Craftsman-Style Bed, but the nut is embedded in the footboard rail tenon rather than in the outside face of the leg.

Side rail

⅜" dowel

Footboard block

T-slot

1½"

1½"

SECTION THROUGH JOINT

Tenon

Bolt hole

Nut

Footboard block

Footboard rail

⁵⁄₁₆" bolt hole

⁵⁄₁₆" square nut

Intersection of footboard rail

in the tenon from the inner side of the rail. Align the nut square to the tenon, and scribe around it with a sharp knife (see **photo F**).

10. Chisel carefully to make the recess (see **photo G** on p. 142). The nut should be just below the surface of the tenon.

11. Test the nut location by threading the bolt through from the opposite side. You could also embed a T-nut, but you have to recess the flange of the T-nut and predrill for each of the prongs that keep it from rotating.

Making the headboard panel

1. Cut a groove ½ in. deep, equal in width to the panel thickness, and ⁵⁄₃₂ in. from the front edge of the lower and crest headboard rails (see "Tenon and Groove Detail for the Crest Rail" on p. 142).

Photo F: Scribe the square nut carefully on the outside cheek of the footboard rail tenon. Wrapping a bit of tape around the bolt before slipping it into the hole in the tenon will help keep you on center.

Photo G: Chisel the recess so the nut fits snugly and drops just below the surface of the tenon.

Tip: *To take the dry-fit frame apart, tap the joints apart from the back side of the headboard using a mallet with a softwood scrap block to keep from marring the wood on the posts.*

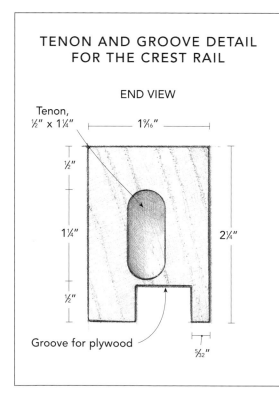

TENON AND GROOVE DETAIL FOR THE CREST RAIL

END VIEW

Tenon, ½" x 1¼"

1⁹⁄₁₆"

½"

1¼"

2¼"

½"

Groove for plywood

⁵⁄₃₂"

2. Check for a good fit on an edge of the plywood piece you'll be using.

3. Dry-assemble the headboard frame, and mark the locations of the grooves in the posts (see **photo H**).

4. Mark the limits of the cut so that they'll be easy to see when you're routing. The grooves in the posts must not go all the way through to either the top or the bottom of the post.

5. Rout the grooves with a plunge router and auxiliary fence. Use the other post for support by clamping it to the bench nearby. Make sure both the post you're working on and the support are clamped securely.

6. Using a ½-in. router bit, rout only about ¹⁄₃₂ in. deep with each pass, until you get to the full depth of ½ in. (see **photo I**).

7. When you've routed a full-depth groove, rotate the workpiece 180 degrees, and reset the fence on the router to give you a dado equal to the thickness of the plywood.

8. Rout the dado to its full width.

9. Dry-assemble the headboard frame, and measure for the panel.

10. Rip and crosscut the panel about ¹⁄₁₆ in. undersize in both dimensions.

11. Test the fit in each of the frame parts individually. Since you tested the fit in the dadoes earlier, you should be very close. You can adjust for an occasional tight spot by sanding the back surface of the panel to ease the fit. Be careful not to sand through the face veneer.

12. Dry-assemble the headboard with the panel in place. Everything should fit together perfectly. If not, make the necessary adjustments and try again.

Grooving the rails to fit the plywood platform

1. On the table saw, cut ½-in. by ¾-in. rabbets on the inside bottom edges of all of the rails to house the edges of the plywood panel.

2. Notch the corners of the plywood so the headboard posts and the footboard blocks will fit. The footboard notches should be 1 in. square. The headboard rail is thicker than the side and footboard rails, so the headboard notches can be ¾ in. by 1 in.

Photo H: Scribe the location for the panel groove in the leg carefully from both the lower and crest rails.

Photo I: The second leg supports the router for cutting the panel groove.

ASSEMBLING THE BED AND FINISHING UP

Gluing up the headboard and footboard

1. Sand all of the surfaces and edges smooth, and chamfer all of the edges.

2. Insert the square nuts into their recesses in the footboard tenons.

3. Get everything you'll need ready, then glue and clamp up the footboard and headboard. Be sparing with the glue; you don't want it oozing into the threads of the nut. Also make sure you don't get glue into the panel groove. It should be free-floating.

Assembling the parts

1. Assemble the base box first, using the special corner bracket hardware. If you're using an inner support structure, slip the two parts together and into place.

2. Lay the platform on top and make sure the cleats all drop inside the box.

3. Now assemble the rails and posts by starting with a side rail and the footboard rail.

4. Insert a bolt and washer into the T-slot, and tighten.

5. Slip this assembly onto the platform.

6. Attach the other side rail.

7. Then attach the headboard. This way, there's no tendency for the headboard to fall over.

Finishing

Apply your choice of finish to all of the bed parts (see Appendix on p. 182 for finishing suggestions).

> *Tip: The assembly sequence for this bed is different from all the others in this book. This way, there's no tendency for the headboard to fall off.*

SLEIGH BED

The idea of a sleigh bed is quite strange indeed. Why make a bed shaped like a sleigh? And why would a bed shaped like a sleigh become so popular? There is no obvious functional connection between the two. In fact, there probably isn't any significant connection at all.

The early versions of this style of bed date from the Greek revival movement of the early 1800s. The overall shapes of this type of bed were fairly common in other types of furniture of the period, especially certain chairs, settees, and what were known as "Grecian couches." These all derive from period interpretations of ancient furniture forms. It was only a small step from couch design to the bed. Did the name come after the style? Most likely. But once coined, the name stuck, even as interpretations varied.

This particular Sleigh Bed is simpler in design than many of the more traditional versions, but the process of building it is nonetheless similar. Making this bed involves many of the basic technical challenges you would find in a more complex design. There are curved legs, which must be cut and smoothed accurately. There are also curved headboard and footboard panels to deal with. Then you must make the joinery on curved parts. This is not difficult, but it falls outside the experience of many woodworkers used to dealing with straight lines.

Sleigh Bed

THE CURVED HEADBOARD AND FOOTBOARD PANELS are laminated on bending forms from thin plywood. The legs and rails are solid wood and cut to shape. Though many parts are curved, all the joinery is cut flat and straight.

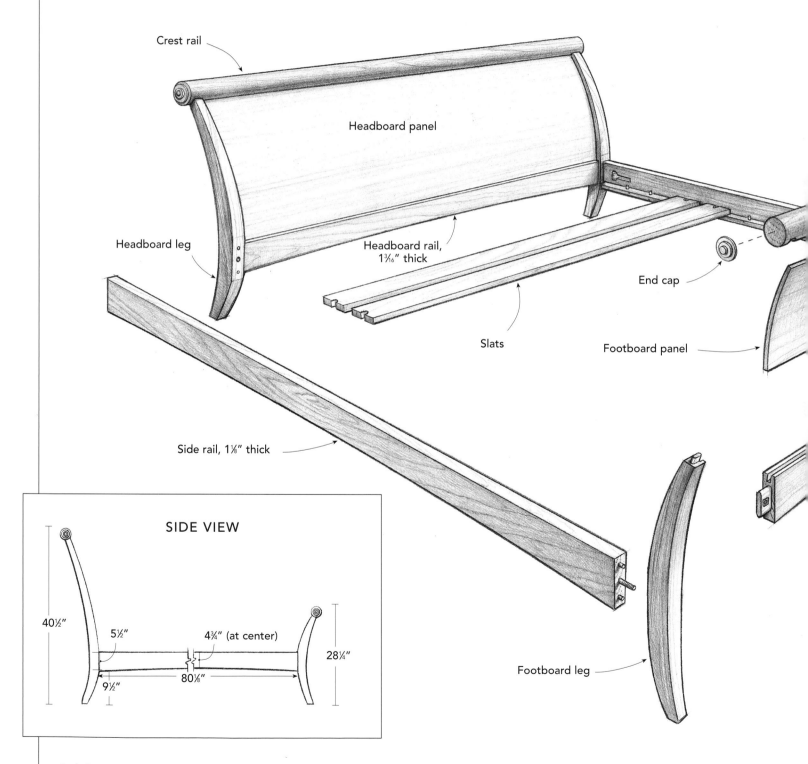

Crest rail

Headboard panel

Headboard leg

Headboard rail, 1¾6" thick

End cap

Slats

Footboard panel

Side rail, 1⅛" thick

Footboard leg

SIDE VIEW

40½"

5½"

4¾" (at center)

28¼"

80⅛"

9½"

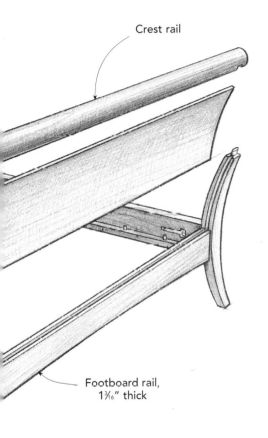

Crest rail

Footboard rail,
1 3/16" thick

HEADBOARD

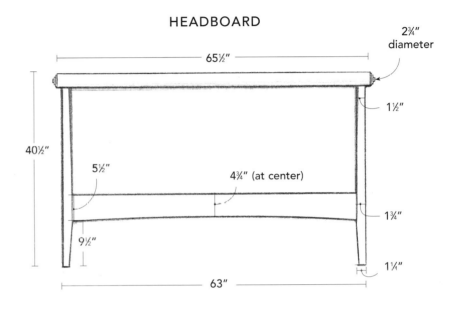

65½"

2¾" diameter

40½"

1½"

5½"

4¾" (at center)

1¾"

9½"

1¼"

63"

FOOTBOARD

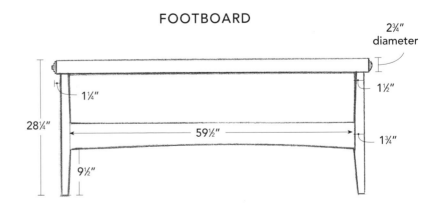

2¾" diameter

1¼"

1½"

28¼"

59½"

1¾"

9½"

BUILDING THE BED STEP-BY-STEP

CUT LIST FOR THE SLEIGH BED

Headboard and Footboard

2	Headboard leg blanks	1¾ in. x 6½ in. x 40 in.
2	Footboard leg blanks	1¾ in. x 5¼ in. x 27¾ in.
1	Curved panel	2 sheets ¼-in. hardwood veneer plywood
2	Headboard and footboard rails	1³⁄₁₆ in. x 5½ in. x 62½ in.
2	Crest rail blanks	2¾ in. x 2¾ in. x 65½ in.
4	Crest rail end cap blanks	2¼ in. x 2¼ in. x ¾ in.

Side Rails

2	Side rails	1⅛ in. x 5½ in. x 80⅛ in.
2	Cleats	1 in. x 1½ in. x 80 in.
16	Slats	¾ in. x 4 in. x 60⅛ in.

Hardware

4	Traditional bed bolts	
8	Dowels (for alignment pins)	⁵⁄₁₆ in. x 1¼ in.
32	Dowels (for locating pins)	⁵⁄₁₆ in. x 1¼ in. or 1½ in.

#6 x 2½-in. screws, as needed

These dimensions are for a queen-size bed. You may have to adjust your dimensions to suit the bed size, the mattress size, or any differences in wood dimensions.

Tip: Be sure to make the flat section longer than the side rail is wide, so that the leg curves begin above and below the side rail joint.

THE MAJOR CHALLENGES on the Sleigh Bed are the curved headboard and footboard panels and the bolster-like crest rails. The panels are laminated from two sheets of ¼-in. plywood; this means making lamination forms but spares any real veneering. The crest rails are actually shaped on the table saw, followed by some handwork.

Start with the legs because their shape determines that of the panels. The panels are next, followed by the rails. Cut the crest rail joinery while it's still just a square blank, since the shaping has little bearing on how the pieces fit together.

MAKING THE LEGS

Making patterns for the legs

1. Enlarge the drawings of the legs to full size (see "Leg Patterns").
2. Transfer the drawings onto some scraps of ¼-in. plywood.
3. Lay out each pattern so the flat area for the side rail is against a flat edge of the pattern stock.
4. Rough-cut the patterns to shape.
5. Work the curves so that they are smooth and fair. Sight down the patterns from both ends, looking for bumps, kinks, or flat spots.
6. Lay out the locations for the mortises on the face of each pattern, and transfer the location lines to the edges of the flat section for the side rail. This will help when you mark the actual legs.

Milling and mortising the legs

The footboard legs are a little easier to get right, so it makes sense to start with them and then to work on the headboard legs.

1. Rip four blanks for the legs from 8/4 stock—two for the headboard that are 6½ in. by 40 in. by 1¾ in. thick and two for the footboard that are 5¼ in. by 27¾ in. by 1¾ in. thick.

2. Joint one edge of the footboard leg blanks, and line up the flat section of the pattern (where the side rail will intersect) with this jointed edge.

3. Carefully mark out the shape of the leg on the blank, then transfer the location of the mortise.

4. Cut the mortise with a plunge router and a fence. For the headboard, angle the pattern so it fits on the 6½-in.-wide blank.

5. Place a straightedge along the flat section of the pattern, and use it to draw a line that extends the flat area in both directions. This will be your reference surface for cutting the mortise in the headboard leg.

6. Bandsaw along this line, then joint or handplane the edge flat and square.

7. Line up the flat section of the pattern along this new edge on the headboard blank, trace the shape, and transfer the mortise location.

8. Cut the mortises.

9. Bandsaw the legs to shape. Save the scrap pieces to use in another step.

10. Smooth the curves, being careful to leave the flat sections untouched (see "Smoothing Curves" on p. 153).

Cutting the tenons on the top of the legs

To hold the crest rails in position, there are tenons on top of all of the legs that run parallel to the curved faces of the legs. Cutting a tenon on the top of a curved part is a difficult proposition, but it's made much easier with a simple positioning block (see "Positioning Block for Cutting the Tenons" on p. 150).

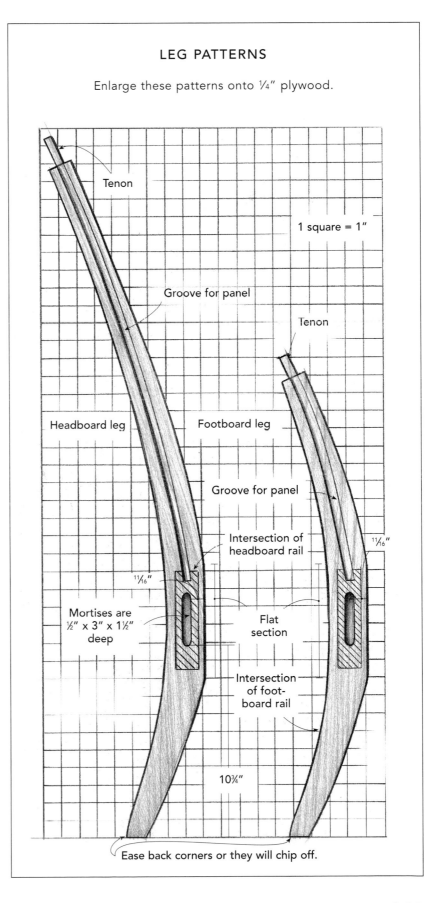

LEG PATTERNS

Enlarge these patterns onto ¼" plywood.

1 square = 1"

Tenon

Groove for panel

Tenon

Headboard leg

Footboard leg

Groove for panel

Intersection of headboard rail

¹¹⁄₁₆"

¹¹⁄₁₆"

Mortises are ½" x 3" x 1½" deep

Flat section

Intersection of footboard rail

10¾"

Ease back corners or they will chip off.

Positioning Block for Cutting the Tenons

The positioning block will hold the leg at the correct angle while the tenon is cut in a jig. This method works for cutting tenons upright on the table saw or with a router and a tenoning jig.

MAKING THE POSITIONING BLOCK

Make up two of these positioning jigs: one for the headboard legs and one for the footboard legs.

1. Lay the leg pattern on a rectangular piece of scrap so the tenon shoulder line is aligned with the square end of the block. The tenon shoulder should be roughly at a right angle to the end of the leg.
2. Trace and cut the curve on the positioning block, and smooth it if necessary.

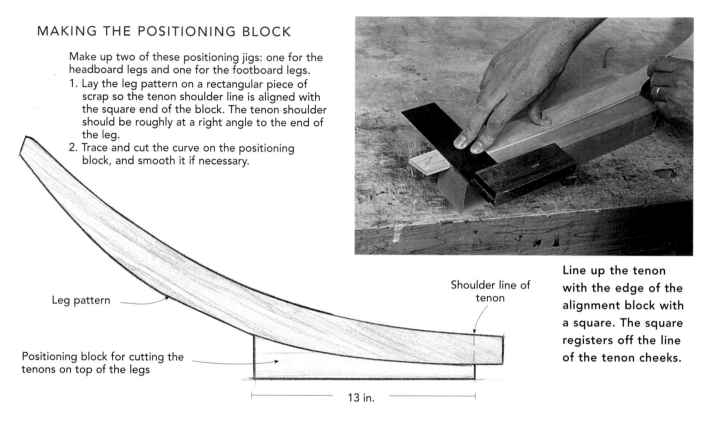

Leg pattern

Shoulder line of tenon

Positioning block for cutting the tenons on top of the legs

13 in.

Line up the tenon with the edge of the alignment block with a square. The square registers off the line of the tenon cheeks.

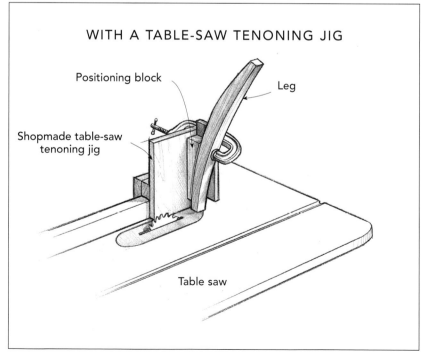

WITH A TABLE-SAW TENONING JIG

Positioning block

Leg

Shopmade table-saw tenoning jig

Table saw

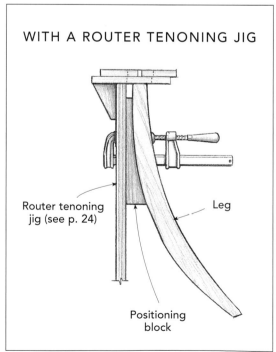

WITH A ROUTER TENONING JIG

Router tenoning jig (see p. 24)

Leg

Positioning block

1. Set up your router or table-saw tenoning jig to cut the tenons in the legs. Attach the alignment block to the jig, and align the end of it with the place where the tenon shoulder will be cut.

2. Clamp the leg in place and cut the tenons.

Cutting the bed bolt joinery

On this bed, use a concealed bed bolt like the one for the Platform Bed. For now, just drill the bolt and alignment holes on the flat sections of, but not through, the legs.

MAKING THE HEADBOARD AND FOOTBOARD

Making lamination forms for the headboard and footboard panels

The remaining work on the legs must wait until the curved panels and the rails are finished. To make the panels, you have to make a set of lamination forms. You can combine the headboard and footboard curves into one larger curve and thereby make one larger set of forms (see "Panel-Bending Forms").

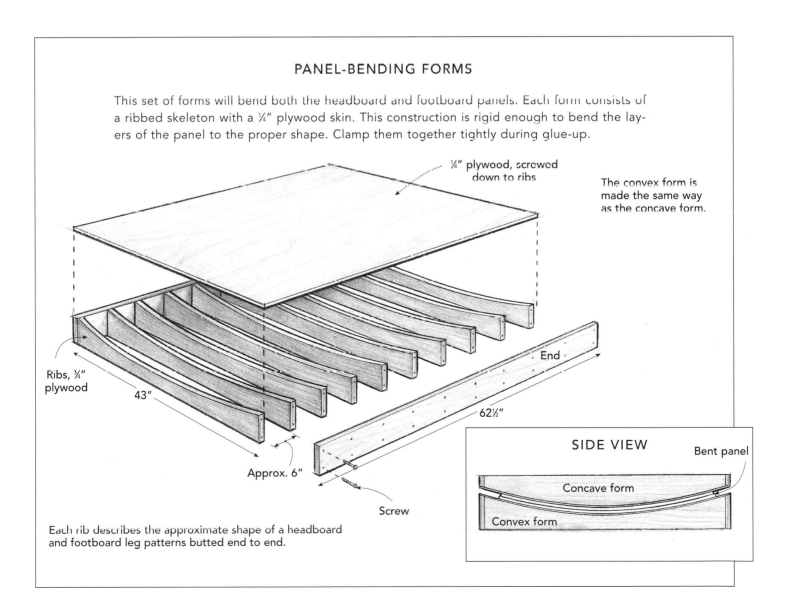

PANEL-BENDING FORMS

This set of forms will bend both the headboard and footboard panels. Each form consists of a ribbed skeleton with a ¼" plywood skin. This construction is rigid enough to bend the layers of the panel to the proper shape. Clamp them together tightly during glue-up.

¼" plywood, screwed down to ribs

The convex form is made the same way as the concave form.

Ribs, ¼" plywood

43"

Approx. 6"

Screw

End

62½"

SIDE VIEW

Bent panel

Concave form

Convex form

Each rib describes the approximate shape of a headboard and footboard leg patterns butted end to end.

Photo A: The single curve for the curved-panel form is made up from the two leg patterns. You can overlap the patterns slightly and line them up so the curve flows from one to the other.

Tip: If you have a vacuum veneer press, you only need to build the bottom half of the form. It will have to be much sturdier however.

1. Align the two leg patterns end to end on a 9-in. by 43-in. piece of ¾-in. plywood to scribe a pattern for the concave ribs (see **photo A**). Keep the curve even and flowing between the patterns.

2. Bandsaw the curve and smooth it.

3. Bandsaw 10 more curved pieces and flush-trim them to match the first. You'll only use a total of 10 to make the form; but you'll need an extra of each type of rib later on for the panel-grooving template.

4. Assemble the lower form, then screw on the ¼-in. plywood skin.

5. To make the complementary form, first determine the thickness of the panel by the thickness of the plywood you use. I've found that two layers of ¼-in. plywood yields a panel ⁷⁄₁₆ in. thick.

6. Make a 1⅜-in.-diameter disk of ¼-in. plywood (equal to the thickness of the panel plus the thickness of the skin on the complementary form), and drill a small hole in the center.

7. Mark out the complementary rib shape by setting the first form on edge on top of a piece of 9-in. by 43-in. plywood. Roll the disk against the form with a pencil in the hole to mark the curve of the ribs for the complementary form (see **photo B**). This is the same technique used for the Windsor Bed forms on p. 119.

8. Build the complementary form to match the first form. Take care to have the ribs line up with each other on both forms.

9. Skin this form with ¼-in. plywood (see **photo C** on p. 154).

Laminating the headboard and footboard panels

To avoid veneering the panels, glue together two sheets of ¼-in. hardwood veneer plywood back to back. Pay attention to the grain and how it will work on the bed (also see "Panel Grain Direction" on p. 154). It takes a bit of preparation—and a bit of clear space—to do this glue-up.

1. Cut two ¼-in. plywood sheets to 42 in. by 60½ in.

2. Gather the materials you'll need for the glue-up, including enough clamps to hold together both ends of each of the ribs and a short-nap paint roller to spread the glue.

3. Set up one of the forms at a convenient height for clamping, for example, on saw-horses or a low bench. You'll want easy access all around for clamping.

4. Lay one of the ¼-in. plywood panels face down on a tarp, some newspaper, or cardboard.

5. Pour a cup or two of glue onto the center of the plywood, and spread it around with the roller, coating the entire surface evenly until it

Photo B: Roll the disk along the completed concave side of the form, keeping the pencil against the near edge of the hole to draw the shape of the mating convex form.

looks wet (see **photo D** on p. 155). Aliphatic resin (typical yellow woodworker's glue) is a good glue for this job. It will probably take about a quart to cover the surface evenly.

6. Place the second ¼-in. plywood panel— good side up—on top of the glued surface, and place both on one side of the form. Then place the mating form on top.

7. Start adding clamps at the center, and work your way out to the ends, alternating sides. It certainly helps to have an assistant for all of this, but you can do it on your own with a lot of running around (see **photo E** on p. 155).

8. When everything is together and tight, let it sit overnight. Don't cut the panels to size just yet.

Tip: When you screw the plywood skins to the ribs, be sure the screws sit below the surface or you'll wind up with indentations on the surface of the panel.

SMOOTHING CURVES

Smoothing convex and concave surfaces takes some patience and the right tools.

For convex surfaces, a handplane or belt sander will work well. Be sure to check often that you're cutting a smooth, even curve.

Concave curves are a little trickier. A compass plane is ideal, but a spokeshave, scraper, and rasp also work well. These tools work better if they are skewed a little. This way their soles or cutting edges don't conform to every bump and hollow from the band-sawn cut.

To finish up, sand with a sanding block made with a curve that is similar to the curve you need to smooth. You'll smooth far more efficiently. To make such a block, just even up some of the waste pieces from cutting the legs to shape.

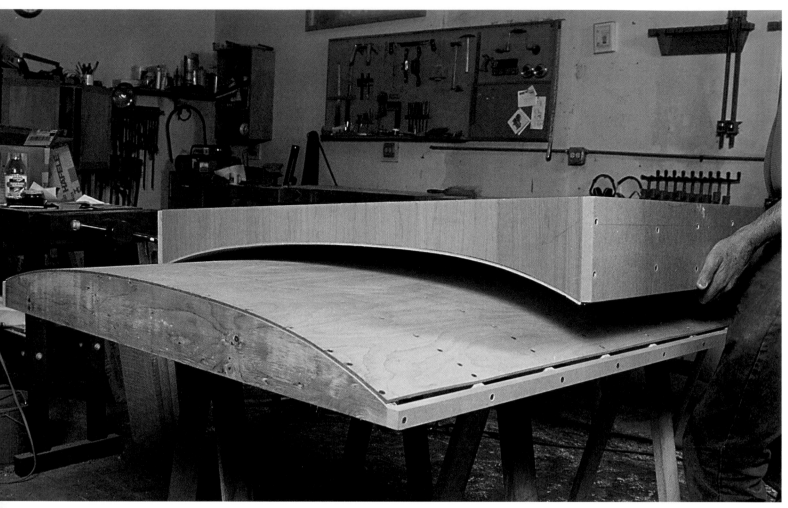

Photo C: The form is larger than either panel but will bend the footboard and headboard panels at once.

PANEL GRAIN DIRECTION

I made this bed with the panel grain running horizontally. The grain direction on a 4 x 8 sheet of plywood demands it. However, it's possible to get what are called 8 x 4 sheets of plywood. These have the grain running the short way and create an up-and-down pattern on the headboard. If you prefer the vertical lines, specialty hardwood plywood dealers should be able to get this for you.

Making the headboard and footboard rails

The main work on the headboard and footboard rails—milling them to size and fitting the hidden bed bolt joint—is routine and covered in more depth in earlier chapters.

1. Mill the rails to 1³⁄₁₆ in. thick, cut them to length, and then cut and fit the tenons. Note that these rails are 5½ in. wide and the 3-in.-wide tenons are centered.

2. Dry-assemble and clamp the legs to the rails.

3. Drill the ³⁄₈-in. bolt hole through the tenon. Be careful not to drill through the outside of the leg. Disassemble the legs and headboard.

4. Insert a ⁵⁄₁₆-in. bolt through the hole in the tenon from the inner side of the rail (a little tape wrapped around the bolt will keep it centered in the hole), and thread a ⁵⁄₁₆-in.-square nut onto it on the outer side of the rail.

5. Scribe the location of the nut, and chisel a recess deep enough to bury the nut just below the surface of the tenon cheek.

6. To lay out the curve on the bottom edge of one of the rails, spring a thin (¼ in. works well) strip of wood so it touches the bottom corners and is at a point ¾ in. up from the bottom in the center of the rail.

7. Trace this curve onto the rail, and bandsaw it to shape. Smooth it out with a skewed handplane, spokeshave, scrapers, and/or sandpaper on a curved sanding block.

8. Trace the finished curve onto the other rail, and cut and smooth it to match.

9. Cut the panel grooves centered in the top edge of the rails about ½ in. deep with a dado blade at an 8 degree angle on the table saw. Size the dadoes for a good fit with the panels.

Photo D: Just pour on the glue and roll it out, making sure to cover every inch. It's hard to see, but I have a sheet of cardboard under the plywood to protect the good face from being marked up on the floor.

Photo E: Start clamping from the middle of the form and work your way to the edges. It may take some running around if you're alone, considering the number of clamps you need.

SLEIGH BED OPTIONS

There is nothing that says you must have curved panels in the headboard and footboard. I like the design better, but it is a fair bit of work. You could opt for a flat panel (and modify the curve of the legs to accommodate it) or make solid-wood slats instead. The slats could be either straight or curved. I won't give specific directions for these other options because they're easy to figure out on your own.

HEADBOARD AND FOOTBOARD OPTIONS

The Sleigh Bed doesn't need curved flat panels to look good. It can also work with curved or straight slats or a flat panel.

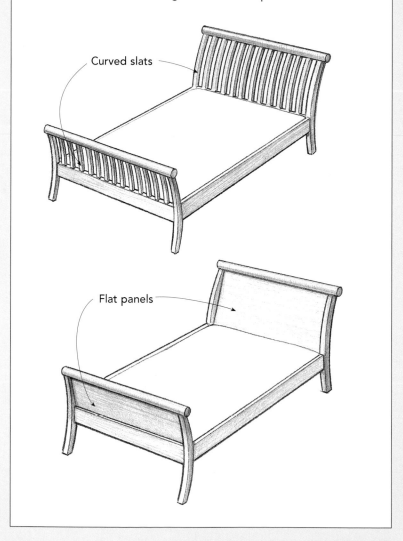

Curved slats

Flat panels

Cutting the crest rail joinery and panel slot

1. Mill up two blanks for the crest rails to 2¾ in. square by 65½ in. long.

2. Determine the exact location for the mortises by clamping up the legs with the lower rail and centering the crest rail blank on the top.

3. Transfer the tenon locations, along with the location for the outside edge of the legs, to a face of the blank (see "Joinery in the Crest Rail Blank").

4. Square these marks across, then lay out the mortise locations centered on the blank.

5. Rout the mortises 1⅝ in. deep using a plunge router with the auxiliary fence attached.

6. Mark out the recesses around the mortises. These should extend from the outside edge of the leg to a line 1½ in. inside. Square these marks across as well.

7. Set the depth of cut on the router to ³⁄₁₆ in. for the footboard crest rail and ⅛ in. for the headboard crest rail.

8. Rout away the waste. Do not cut over the line on either end; however, you can rout all the way off the sides, because this wood will be cut off anyhow.

9. Rout the ½-in.-deep slot for the panel the whole length from mortise to mortise. The width of this slot is determined by the actual width of your panel and should be centered on the rail. It does not need to be angled at 8 degrees the way the slots in the rails were.

10. Fit the tenons on the ends of the legs to these mortises as best you can. You won't be able to fit the joints completely just yet because you haven't tapered the legs yet.

11. Scribe the location of the groove from the crest rail onto the legs.

Tip: Make sure you don't have any glue on the outside surface of the panel or forms. If you do, you'll glue the forms and panels together. Wax the outside edges of the forms before glue-up to prevent problems.

Joinery in the Crest Rail Blank

The leg joins the crest rail blank in a double mortise, the shallow one called a recess. Cut the joinery in the crest rail before you shape it because clamping and routing flat surfaces is much easier than on curved surfaces.

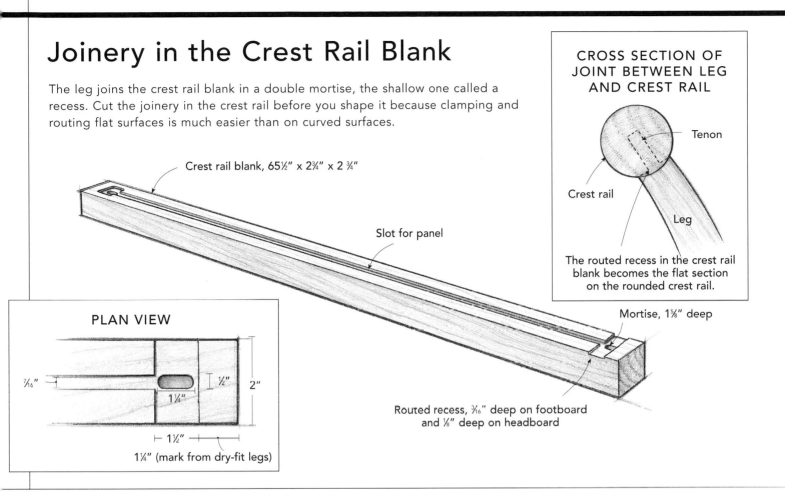

Crest rail blank, 65½" x 2¾" x 2 ¾"

Slot for panel

CROSS SECTION OF JOINT BETWEEN LEG AND CREST RAIL

Tenon

Crest rail

Leg

The routed recess in the crest rail blank becomes the flat section on the rounded crest rail.

Mortise, 1⅝" deep

PLAN VIEW

⁷/₁₆"

½"

2"

1¼"

1½"

1¼" (mark from dry-fit legs)

Routed recess, ³/₁₆" deep on footboard and ⅛" deep on headboard

Making the rails cylindrical

The cylindrical crest rails (which look like round bolsters) are one of the nicest aspects of this bed. I don't have a lathe with a 62-in. capacity to turn them, and I suspect you don't either. I found that the easiest way to make them is by hand. Cutting a 16-sided polygon is not all that difficult, and from there, shaping to round isn't such a big deal at all. This is a technique used to make masts for wooden boats.

1. Lay out an octagon inside a square that is the exact size of your crest rail blanks (see "Two Octagon Layout Methods" on p. 61).
2. Transfer the octagon to an end of the blank.
3. Set up your table saw to cut a 45 degree angle, and cut the sides of the octagon. You may want to sneak up on the perfect octagon

by cutting a little outside your layout lines and moving in until the width of each facet is almost identical in width (see **photo F** on p. 158).
4. Set the saw angle to 22½ degrees and the rip fence to take off a tiny bit of each corner on the octagon until all the facets are of equal width (see **photo G** on p. 158). Be careful: The rail can twist easily in the cut because there isn't a large flat surface registering against the fence.
5. Though the rail is already pretty close to round, there's plenty of handwork to do yet. Set the blank on a workbench, and try to plane or sand it to a 32-sided polygon (see **photo H** on p. 159).
6. Sand the rail round with a concave sanding block. Make the block by cutting out a 2¹³/₁₆-in. curve on an appropriately sized piece of scrap (see **photo I** on p. 159). Work your way up to 220 grit.

Tip: You don't need 32 absolutely equal sides here, but thinking that you do will keep your cuts evenly distributed around the rail and get you that much closer to a really round crest rail.

Grooving the legs for the panels

Since it's easier to work on the legs when they are still flat, groove the panels before you cut the taper on their inside faces.

1. Make a grooving template for a router (see "Panel-Grooving Template" on p. 160). This template will work on one of the headboard legs and the opposite corner footboard leg. You'll need to reverse the template to cut the other two.

2. Test your setup before routing the grooves because the dimensions given are based on a panel thickness of $7/16$ in. Adjust the template to correct for too much or too little room so that it cuts a groove your panel will fit into snugly.

3. Locate the template on one of the legs, using the marks you made on the leg from the lower and crest rail grooves. These are the marks that were made on the legs when test-

Photo F: Ripping the four corners off the crest rail blank at 45 degrees will make an octagon. Don't let the tilting table in the photo throw you off. A more common tilting arbor saw will also do the job.

Photo G: Cut the corners off the octagon to produce a 16-sided polygon. Note: the author moves his left hand out of the way of the blade before pushing the rail through the cut. Keep an eye on the location of your hands when you cut these rails.

Photo H: Handplane all the edges to produce a 32-sided polygon, which is getting very close to round. The handwork is fun at this point.

Photo I: A curved sanding block and some 80- or 100-grit sandpaper are the keys to getting the rail round. Once you're satisfied with the shape, use finer grits to smooth the rail.

fitting the lower and crest rails. The grooves in the legs need to meet up with them exactly. Clamp the template to the leg.

4. Plunge-rout the first two grooves, cutting only about 1/32 in. of depth per pass. Continue until the grooves are about 3/8 in. deep (see **photo J** on p. 161).

5. Screw another piece of 1/4-in. plywood to the top of the template.

6. Remove the first piece of plywood, and flip the jig over. You'll have to rout through the new plywood so you can set up the jig in the proper position on the legs.

7. Rout the remaining grooves.

8. Test-fit the panels in the legs. If the fit is not perfect, you can sand a little bit off the panel—but don't sand through a layer of veneer. If you have to, reset the template to rout a slightly wider groove.

Sizing the panels

Now that sections of the panel fit into the grooves, you can get an accurate size for cutting the panels to width.

1. Fit a leg onto the appropriate section of the uncut panel, and then figure the depths of the grooves in the lower and crest rails.

Tip: A curved panel is very dangerous to cut on the table saw, so don't even think about it.

Panel-Grooving Template

The template is simply two extra ribs from the panel-bending forms, screwed to a piece of plywood. The router is guided using a ¾" guide bushing and a ¼" router bit, and will cut a ⁷⁄₁₆" wide groove.

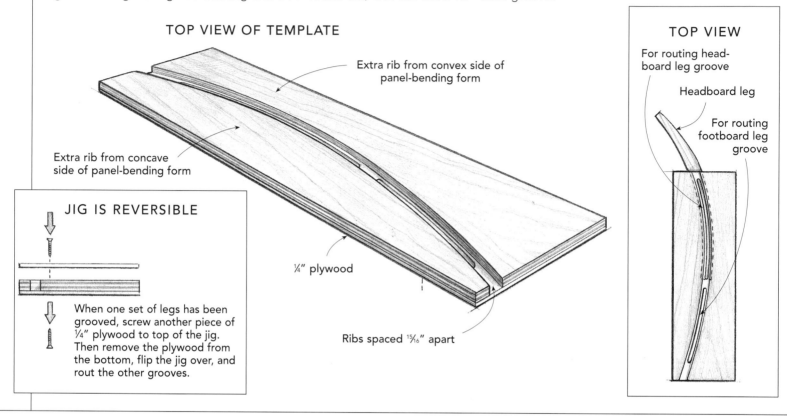

TOP VIEW OF TEMPLATE

Extra rib from convex side of panel-bending form

Extra rib from concave side of panel-bending form

¼" plywood

Ribs spaced ¹⁵⁄₁₆" apart

JIG IS REVERSIBLE

When one set of legs has been grooved, screw another piece of ¼" plywood to top of the jig. Then remove the plywood from the bottom, flip the jig over, and rout the other grooves.

TOP VIEW

For routing head-board leg groove

Headboard leg

For routing footboard leg groove

---

2. Mark the panel, and cut it to size with a portable jigsaw.
3. Sand the rough edges smooth, but don't get too carried away because they'll be buried in the groove anyhow.

Tapering the inside faces of the legs

The last real work you need to do to the legs is to taper them above and below the flat area where the rail meets the leg.

1. Mark out the taper, starting about 1 in. above and below the flat area.
2. Cut the tapers on the bandsaw, convex side down. Be careful to keep the part you are cutting down flat on the saw table.

3. Plane the tapers smooth. Ease the transitions from taper to flat so they change gradually, without a hard edge.

Fitting the legs to the crest rail

1. Fit the tops of the legs and the bottom of the crest rails to form a seamless joint.
2. If necessary, reshape the upper part of the legs slightly to fit against the recessed flat without any overhang. If the legs are a little too narrow, sand the area around the flat on the crest rail a little to hide the discrepancy.
3. Round over the edges of the legs slightly—I used a ⅛-in. roundover bit—and chamfer or ease the edges on the rails. Stop about 1 in. below the top of each leg. You'll work on this transition after assembly.

Photo J: The leg and template are set up for the curved groove to be routed.

Assembling the headboard and footboard

1. Do a final test fitting, and smooth away all the various dents and nicks that come with a project sitting around in the shop.

2. Put a quick coat of finish on the curved panels. This way, if there's any shifting around, you won't see a line of unfinished wood.

3. Insert the headboard panel into the lower headboard rail groove.

4. Spread some glue in the leg mortises and very lightly on the rail tenons. The panel doesn't get any glue at all. Don't forget to put the square nuts in place in the recesses in the tenons.

5. Put the legs on the rail, and clamp slowly, watching carefully that the panel slides into its groove. You should only need one or two 6-ft. bar clamps (with pads).

6. Clamp up tight, and put this assembly safely to one side while you do the other.

7. Repeat this process for the footboard.

8. Make a caul to help you clamp the crest rails onto the legs because the round surface and the curved legs don't offer any easy clamping purchase. The caul I use resembles an open-ended trough. It slips over the round upper rail and gives a flat surface to clamp on (see **photo K** on p. 162).

9. Spread glue into the mortises and lightly on the tenons, and slip the rail on. You need

clamps on both sides of the caul so that you can exert even clamping pressure. Your best bet is to clamp to the underside of the headboard or footboard rail.

10. Clamp very slowly and watch to be sure the panel goes easily into its groove. It's usually easier to work one end down a bit ahead of the other, so you're not trying to slip the entire edge of the panel into place all at once.

11. Take the clamps off carefully when the glue has set. Loosening one side tends to allow the clamps on the other side to slip off.

12. Fair in the transition from the rounded-over part of the leg to the point where the leg and the crest rail meet (see **photo L**).

FINISHING TOUCHES

Making the side rails

The side rails are blessedly uncomplicated, and so I consider them a finishing touch rather than a substantial step.

1. Mill the rails to 5½ in. wide, 1⅛ in. thick, and 80⅛ in. long.

Photo K: To clamp the rail to the headboard, a trough-like caul is essential. It helps give you enough pressure where you need it during glue-up.

Photo L: Finish-sand the rounded edges of the legs all the way up to the crest rail. You can also ease the transition between the underside of the rail and the flat section if the leg and rail don't meet perfectly.

2. Drill the ends for the bed bolt in the center and the two alignment dowels to either side of it.

3. Rout a T-shaped recess for the bolts on the inside face at each end of the rail. Locate the recess 4 in. from the end of the rail. The same joint is described in detail in the Craftsman Style Bed on p. 109.

4. Mark out, cut, and smooth the arch on the bottom edge of both rails just as you did for the headboard and footboard rails.

5. Chamfer or ease all of the edges.

Making the cleats and slats

1. Mill the cleats 1 in. by 1½ in. by 80 in. long—just less than the length of the side rails.

2. Drill the ⁵⁄₁₆-in. holes for the locating pins about ¾ in. deep in one of the 1-in.-wide sides of the cleat. These holes are spaced every 5 in., starting 2½ in. from each end.

3. Clamp the cleats into place on the side rails, so the top edge of the cleat is just touching the bottom edge of the T-slot.

4. Mark the curve of the bottom of the rail on the cleat, and bandsaw and smooth to shape.

5. Drill countersunk pilot holes for the screws that will attach the cleats to the rails on an adjacent face of the cleat. These holes should be spaced roughly 6 in. apart and should be staggered up and down on the ends, where there is room.

6. Glue ⁵⁄₁₆-in. by 1¼-in.- to 1½-in.-long dowels into each of the ⁵⁄₁₆-in. holes.

7. Set the cleats aside. Don't attach them until after you've applied finish to the rails.

8. Mill 16 slats ¾ in. by 4 in., and cut them to a length that fits the space between the rails.

9. Cut notches in the ends of the slats to fit over the dowel pins in the cleats. See "Table-Saw Notching Jig" on p. 34 for a more complete discussion cutting notches in slats.

Making and attaching the crest rail end caps

You might want to dress up the ends of the crest rails with some sort of ornamentation.

END CAP DETAIL

END VIEW

End of crest rail

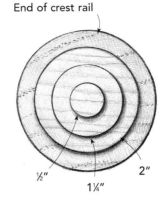

½" 1¼" 2"

SIDE VIEW

End cap

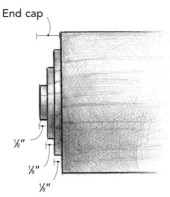

⅛"
⅛"
⅛"

End caps add a nice detail and are easy to turn. I applied glue, aligned them in the center, then held them in place with masking tape.

1. Turn four little caps for the ends and glue them into place (see "End Cap Detail").

2. "Size" the mating surfaces between the end cap and the crest rails, which means to apply some slightly diluted glue. The size coat fills the end grain pores, giving the glue a solid surface to mate with. Remember that these glue joints won't see a whole lot of stress, so they shouldn't have trouble holding.

Finishing

Apply your choice of finish to all of the bed parts (see Appendix on p. 182 for finishing suggestions).

Tip: Don't get glue outside of the area where the decorative caps will go because it will affect the penetration of the finish.

BUNK BEDS

Stacking beds on top of one another was originally a way to make room for more people to sleep on a boat. But this purely practical way to get extra sleeping space in tight quarters has developed into what most kids consider pure fun. Whether you need to cram in some extra sleeping space or just want to create a fun way for kids to share a room, bunk beds are a terrific solution.

Even if you are building bunk beds just for the fun of it, there is one very important issue that needs to be addressed: safety. Bunk beds can be dangerous for kids. This bed is designed with federal safety guidelines in mind (see "Bunk Bed Safety" on p. 177), and any variation you might consider should follow them carefully as well.

Admittedly, this is not a simple project just because it's a bunk bed. I designed this bed for its appearance in addition to its functionality. You could make the project easier in lots of different ways. Don't skimp on the safety features, however.

Bear in mind that you don't have to consider this a desgin that will work solely for bunk beds, either. You could easily use this basic look to build an elegant nonstacking bed of any size.

Bunk Beds

THESE BUNK BEDS are fairly typical in construction, but there's a lot more to them than to a one-level bed, including over 100 spindles. The side rails join to the headboard and footboard assemblies with bolts and barrel nuts. The guardrails are held in place with mortise-and-tenon joints. The ladder attaches to the top bunk with a hook-and-slot type of bed-rail fastener.

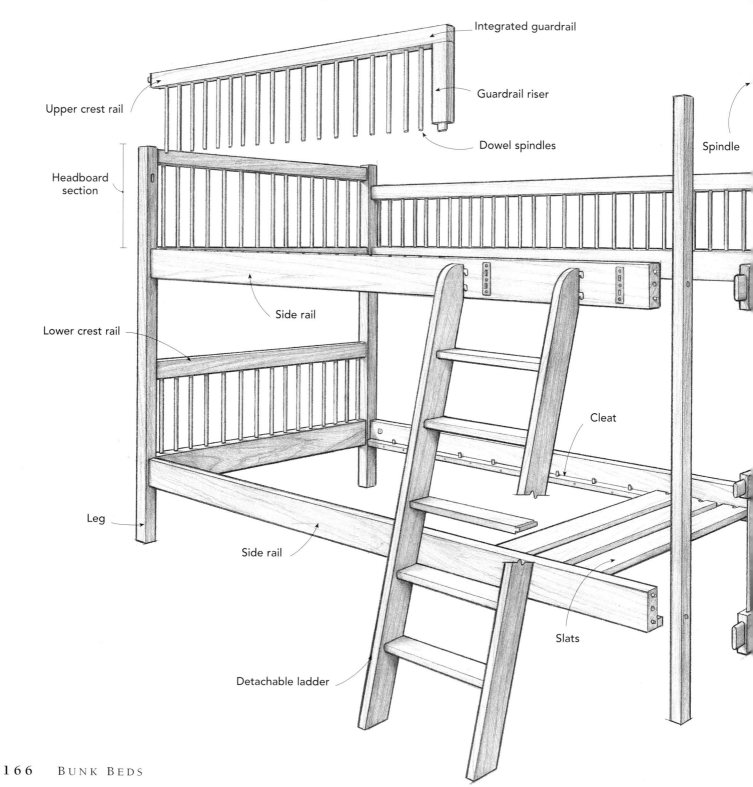

Integrated guardrail

Guardrail riser

Upper crest rail

Dowel spindles

Spindle

Headboard section

Side rail

Lower crest rail

Cleat

Leg

Side rail

Slats

Detachable ladder

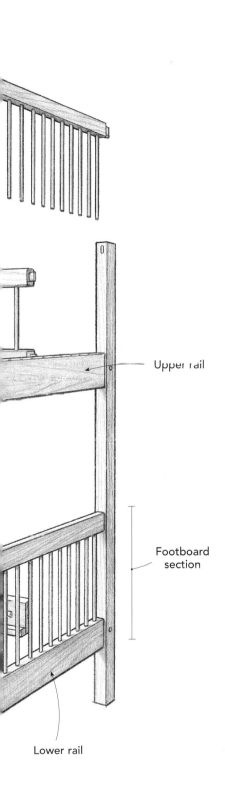

Upper rail

Footboard section

Lower rail

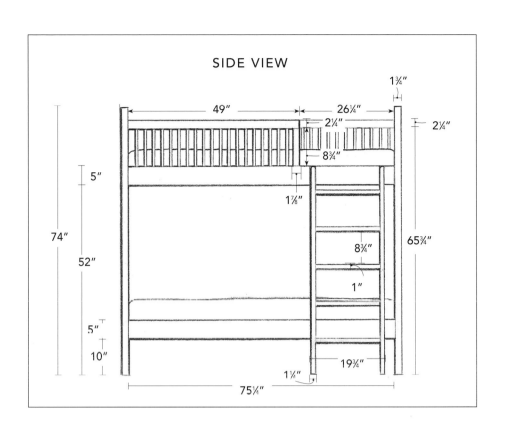

SIDE VIEW

1¾"

49"   26¼"

2¼"

2¼"

8¾"

5"

1⅞"

74"

52"

8¾"

65¾"

1"

5"

10"

19¾"

1¼"

75¼"

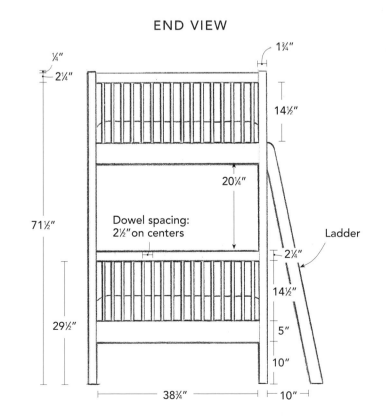

END VIEW

1¾"

¼"

2¼"

14½"

20¼"

71½"

Dowel spacing: 2½" on centers

2¼"

Ladder

14½"

29½"

5"

10"

38¾"   10"

BUILDING THE BED STEP-BY-STEP

CUT LIST FOR BUNK BEDS

Legs and Rails

4	Legs	1¾ in. x 1¾ in. x 74 in.
4	Headboard and footboard rails	1⁵⁄₁₆ in. x 5 in. x 41¾ in.
4	Side rails	1⁵⁄₁₆ in. x 5 in. x 75¼ in.
4	Crest rails	1⁵⁄₁₆ in. x 2¼ in. x 41¾ in.
1	Rear guardrail	1⁵⁄₁₆ in. x 2¼ in. x 78¼ in.
1	Front guardrail	1⁵⁄₁₆ in. x 2¼ in. x 50½ in.
1	Front guardrail riser	1⁵⁄₁₆ in. x 1⅞ in. x 10¾ in.
64	Headboard and footboard spindles	⅝ in. x 16⅜ in.
50	Guardrail spindles	⅝ in. x 10⅝ in.

Mattress Support

4	Cleats	1 in. x 1¼ in. x 75⅛ in.
30	Slats	¾ in. x 4 in. x 39⅛ in.

Ladder Parts

2	Ladder uprights	1¼ in. x 2⅞ in. x 58½ in.
6	Ladder rungs	1 in. x 2⅞ in. x 18¼ in.

Hardware

8	Barrel nuts and bolts	
16	Dowels (for alignment pins)	⁵⁄₁₆ in. by 1¼ in. long
2	Bed-rail fasteners	
60	Dowels (for locating pins)	⁵⁄₁₆ in. by 1½ in. long

#6 x 1⅝-in. screws, as needed

Bunk beds are not normally made in any size but twin. This unit is made with the top and bottom bunks attached. It has integral guardrails and a detachable ladder.

BASIC CONSTRUCTION of the bunk beds is similar to the other beds in this book. Time-wise, keep in mind that you have to cut more joints because you are making two beds at once. The side rails for the bunk bed differ only in the fastener used to attach them to the legs. The top bunk side rails incorporate the guardrails. The ladder comes last because you need dimensions from the rest of the bed to build it to fit well.

MAKING THE BED FRAME PARTS

Making the legs

I chose barrel nuts to fasten the rails to the legs on these beds. As all joinery systems for beds are, barrel nuts are a compromise (see "Barrel Nuts vs. Bed Bolt Nuts" on p. 170). Choose the nuts before you make the legs because they require different size bolt holes.

1. Mill and cut the stock for the legs to size.
2. Lay out and cut the various mortises on the legs with whatever mortising tools you prefer (see "Leg Mortise Details").
3. Drill the holes for the bolts and alignment dowels (see p. 49 for a discussion of drilling these holes).
4. If you use ⅜-in. barrel nuts and bolts, you'll need a larger (⅞ in.) counterbore and bolt hole. Just drill ⅜-in. holes with the doweling jig, and then enlarge them with a ¹³⁄₃₂-in. bit, letting the drill follow the hole.

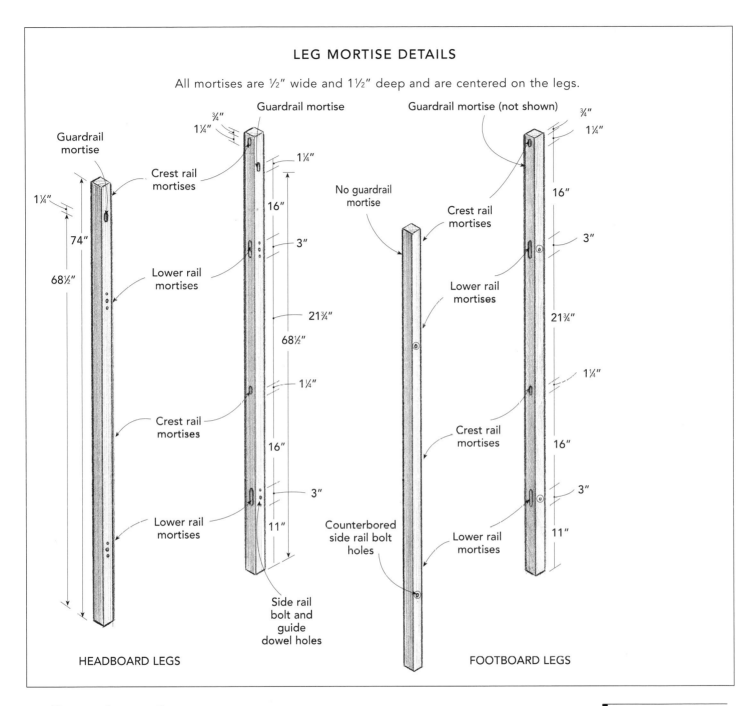

LEG MORTISE DETAILS

All mortises are ½" wide and 1½" deep and are centered on the legs.

Guardrail mortise

Guardrail mortise (not shown)

Guardrail mortise

¾"

1¼"

Crest rail mortises

Crest rail mortises

No guardrail mortise

Crest rail mortises

1¼"

1¼"

74"

68½"

Lower rail mortises

16"

3"

21¾"

68½"

Lower rail mortises

¾"

1¼"

16"

3"

21¾"

Crest rail mortises

16"

Crest rail mortises

1¼"

16"

3"

1¼"

Lower rail mortises

Counterbored side rail bolt holes

3"

11"

Side rail bolt and guide dowel holes

Lower rail mortises

11"

HEADBOARD LEGS

FOOTBOARD LEGS

Milling the rails

1. Mill the headboard, footboard, side, and guardrail stock 1⁵⁄₁₆ in. thick if you're using barrel nuts. If you choose the hardware store bolt system used on most of the other beds, you can mill the rails up to 1⅛ in. or even 1¹⁄₁₆ in. thick.

2. Rip the side and lower rails to 5 in. wide and the crest rails and guardrails to 2¼ in. wide. The guardrail riser should be 1⅞ in. wide.

3. Cut the headboard and footboard rails to length based on the cut list lengths. If the thicknesses vary from those in the drawing on pp. 166-167, calculate the lengths on the thicknesses of the parts you've made (see the formula on p. 11).

4. Cut the side rails to length.

Tip: Be sure to mark out each leg clearly for both position and orientation, so you won't lose track of what joint goes where in the middle of the whole process.

Cutting the rail tenons

1. Cut and fit all of the tenons to their mortises, in whatever manner you prefer. The setup for cutting all rail tenons is the same, since all are centered on the rails and are ½ in. thick.

2. Mark each joint as you fit it with a unique letter or number.

3. Test-assemble the headboard and footboard framework.

4. While the frames are together, measure the distance between the lower rail and the crest rail on the headboard and footboard on both top and bottom beds. You'll need this information when you cut the spindles to length.

Drilling the side rails for the barrel nut joinery

1. Drill the bolt holes carefully, using a ⅜-in. drill bit guided by a self-centering doweling

Tip: If you drill the barrel nut holes as deep as possible and they still don't line up with the bolt holes, file down the inside face of the barrel nut.

BARREL NUTS VS. BED BOLT NUTS

There is a theoretical advantage to using barrel nuts over hardware store nuts and bolts or traditional bed bolts. You can simply drill a hole in the inside face of the side rail to install the nuts, instead of chiseling or routing the nut recess.

Achieving the required accuracy is actually quite different, and you'll need to use thicker rails for the barret nuts to work. You'll also have to drill larger holes and larger counterbores through the legs to accommodate the larger bolt size. Finally, barrel nuts are harder to find and more costly.

The basic setup for the barrel nut and bolt is the same as for hex-head bolts and nuts, but you can just drill a hole instead of chiseling or routing a flat internal surface for a regular nut. The bolt hole and the nut hole must meet perfectly, however.

jig. You may have to deepen the hole a little once the jig is removed, so that the bolt hole is about $3\frac{3}{4}$ in. deep.

2. Drill the two holes for the alignment dowels with a $\frac{5}{16}$-in. bit, again guided by the doweling jig.

3. Enlarge the bolt hole with a $\frac{13}{32}$-in. drill bit (for the $\frac{3}{8}$-in. bolts used with the barrel nuts).

4. Set up a drill press to drill the holes for the barrel nuts on the inside faces of the rails. Use a $\frac{3}{4}$-in. Forstner bit for this because you need a $1\frac{3}{16}$-in.-deep hole in the $1\frac{5}{16}$-in.-thick rail, and you don't want a guide point to come through the outside face of the rail.

5. Drill the holes centered on the width of the rail and $3\frac{3}{16}$ in. from the ends. Test the holes to be sure you can thread the bolt onto the nut.

6. Smooth all of the rail surfaces, and chamfer the edges of all of the rails.

Making the guardrails

The guardrails are attached to the side rails by the spindles. Tenons on the ends of the guardrail seat in mortises in the legs but are not glued in. The bolted rail joint holds things together just fine. You can also build the guardrails as detachable frames instead of as an integral part of the side rails (see "Detachable Guardrails" on p. 172).

1. Cut the rear guardrail to $78\frac{1}{4}$ in. long. Cut the front guardrail to 49 in. This will leave a space in this rail so you can climb up and down from the top bunk.

2. Cut $1\frac{1}{2}$-in.-long tenons on both ends of the rear guardrail and on one end of the front guardrail to match the mortises in the legs. Make sure that the length of the rear guardrail between its tenon shoulders is exactly the same length as the side rail.

3. Tenon the front guardrail riser into the appropriate side rail, cutting a 1-in.-long tenon.

4. Join the front guardrail to this riser using either a mortise-and-tenon or half-lap joint. (You'll need a longer riser for the half lap.)

5. Wax the guardrail tenons so they go together and come apart easily when they knock down with the side rails. Don't wax the riser tenons—these will be glued.

Drilling for the spindles

Lay out the centers for all of the spindle holes in all of the rails by clamping pairs of rails together and measuring and marking with a square across both. This way you're sure that the matched holes will line up in each sub-assembly.

1. Set up a fence on a drill press to drill all of the holes in the center of the rails.

2. Screw some blocks to the bottom of your drill press fence, to support the long rails when you drill near the ends. A separate support stand works even better.

3. Set the depth stop on the drill press to about 1 in. deep for all of the holes.

4. Drill some $\frac{5}{8}$-in. test holes in a scrap of the same material you're using on the bed. Test-fit more than a few dowels to make sure you're using the right size bit (see "16mm Holes for $\frac{5}{8}$-in. Dowels").

Tip: Check your setup before you drill each hole— sawdust between the fence and the workpiece or a bow in the wood can push the edge of the rail away from the fence and cause you to drill off center.

16MM HOLES FOR $\frac{5}{8}$-IN. DOWELS

Though there's some variation in size between $\frac{5}{8}$-in. drill bits, I've found that they generally drill holes too small to fit $\frac{5}{8}$-in. dowels, which tend to be slightly oversize. If the bit you have drills holes too small, it will be well worth your time to buy a 16mm bit. It's available from any local machinist's supply house.

16mm bits are 0.00492 in. larger than $\frac{5}{8}$ in. and will save you hours of time fitting $\frac{5}{8}$-in. dowels to the holes. However, always test your dowels before drilling all the holes. A batch of undersize $\frac{5}{8}$-in. dowels will be loose and rattle around in 16mm holes. You may also want to try the dowel shrinking technique used for the Windsor Bed on p. 128.

DETACHABLE GUARDRAILS

Detachable guardrails should be built as four-sided frames, with the spindles running between the crest and lower rails. Join the rails and stiles with mortise-and-tenon joints (or whatever you prefer). Then lay out the dowel holes on the crest and lower rails, drill, and fit the spindles in place.

The guardrails should be attached to both the headboard and footboard legs with ⅜-in. dowels. They should also be screwed to the side rails with a 1-in. L-shaped aluminum channel along the bottom edge. I've suggested 11 in. for the height of the guard rails, but be sure to leave at least 5 in. above the mattress.

REAR GUARDRAIL

Guardrails can be made detachable by adding a frame on all four sides that connects in a knockdown fashion to the side rails.

Dowel, ⅜" and 1" down from top edge, fits into matching hole in leg.

1¾"

2½" on centers

11"

2"

75⅛"

FRONT GUARDRAIL

Dowel, ⅜" in headboard end only

2"

1¾"

11"

49"

GUARDRAIL ATTACHMENT

1⁵⁄₁₆"

Screw 1" L-shaped aluminum channel into the bottom of the guardrail and to the inside of the side rail.

5. Drill all of the holes, relying on your eye as much as the fence to ensure that the holes do in fact wind up on target.

6. Cut the spindles to length. For the exact lengths of the spindles, add the actual hole depths to the distance between the rails that you measured when the headboard and footboard were test-assembled, then subtract ⅛ in. The extra ⅛ in. leaves room for any excess glue in the joint.

7. Check the fit of every spindle in every hole. It's better to discover a problem now before there's glue setting in the joint.

ASSEMBLING THE HEADBOARD, FOOTBOARD, AND SIDE RAILS

Assembly comes into two parts. First, you make the headboard, footboard, and side rail subassemblies. These each consist of upper and lower rails connected with spindles. Then you attach the headboard and footboard subassemblies to the legs.

Assembling the subassemblies

The main concern in this first assembly step is keeping the distances between rails and crest rails constant.

1. Cut four or five blocks of scrapwood to the exact distance you want between the rails. Hold these between the rails while clamping up, to keep them the right distance apart.

2. Spread a little bit of glue in each of the holes on one of the rails.

3. Insert the dowels into the holes all the way, then spread glue in the holes in the corresponding rail, and work the dowels in place one at a time.

4. Clamp the crest rail and lower rail together to seat the dowels, using the blocks to control the distance between the rails (see **photo A** on p. 173).

5. Repeat this procedure for the top and bottom sections of the headboards and footboards as well as for the two top side rail/guardrail assemblies.

Gluing up the headboard and footboard assemblies

1. Check to be sure that the tenons on each of the headboard and footboard sections are the right distance apart to fit in the leg mortises. Pare or rasp a little bit off the tenon if necessary.

2. Glue and clamp the lower and upper footboard rail subassemblies to the legs. You will need a minimum of four 4-ft.-long clamps.

3. Do the same with the headboard subassemblies and the headboard legs.

Making the cleats and slats

1. Make cleats and slats for both the upper and lower beds as for the First Bed (see p. 31).

2. For extra security, use $5/16$-in. by $1\frac{1}{2}$-in.-long dowels in the cleats instead of $1\frac{1}{4}$-in.-long ones. The dowels will project up above the notched slots, helping to keep everything in place during those outlawed trampoline sessions.

Assembling the bunk bed

1. Attach a bottom side rail to either the headboard or footboard of the bed, then loosely attach the other end.

2. Tighten the bolt and nut only enough to make sure the joint doesn't fall apart. This will leave room to get the top side rail into place.

3. Move on to the other side, where the same considerations apply.

4. Tighten all of the bolts securely once you have all of the rails in place.

MAKING THE LADDER

Milling the rungs and sides

You don't have to make an angled ladder, but I like both the look and the greater ease of climbing that it provides.

1. Mill up the stock for the ladder uprights to $1\frac{1}{4}$ in. thick by $2\frac{7}{8}$ in. wide by $58\frac{1}{2}$ in. long. The rungs should be 1 in. thick by $2\frac{7}{8}$ in. wide by $18\frac{1}{4}$ in. long.

2. Determine the angle of the ladder by laying out the critical dimensions on a piece of plywood that's at least 13 in. by 60 in. (see "Angles for the Ladder Sides").

3. Set a bevel gauge from the angle you've drawn on the plywood, and transfer this angle to the miter gauge on your table saw.

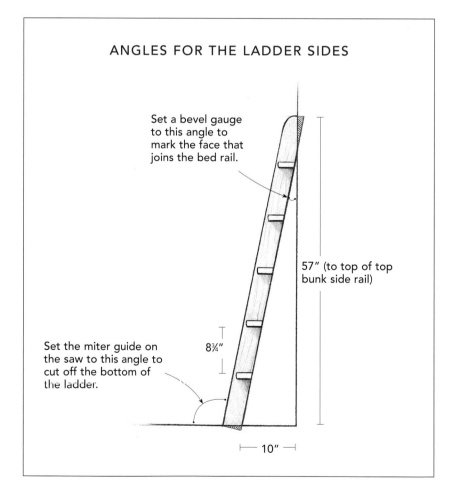

ANGLES FOR THE LADDER SIDES

Set a bevel gauge to this angle to mark the face that joins the bed rail.

57" (to top of top bunk side rail)

Set the miter guide on the saw to this angle to cut off the bottom of the ladder.

8¾"

10"

Jig for Routing Dovetail Slots

This jig ensures that all of the angles are correct on both sides of the ladder and that all of the dovetail slots are identical. It also makes it easy to cut stopped dovetail grooves, so the dovetails don't show on the front edge.

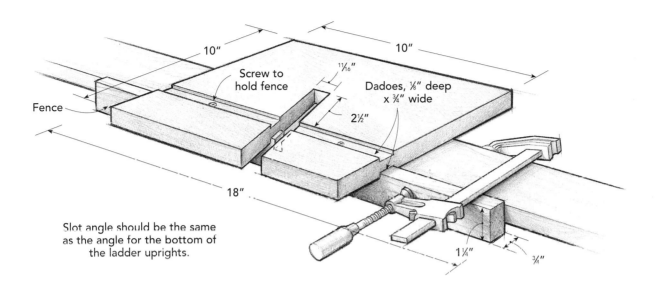

10"

10"

Screw to
hold fence

$^{11}\!/_{16}$"

Dadoes, $^{1}\!/_{8}$" deep
x $^{3}\!/_{4}$" wide

Fence

2½"

18"

Slot angle should be the same
as the angle for the bottom of
the ladder uprights.

1¼"

$^{3}\!/_{4}$"

BUILDING THE JIG

Use a scrap of 10" x 10" plywood or MDF.
1. Set your table-saw miter gauge to the angle you cut the bottoms of the ladder uprights.
2. Make a series of stopped cuts to create an $^{11}\!/_{16}$" wide slot, about 5" long.
3. Bandsaw or file the end of the slot flat and perpendicular to the sides.
4. Cut identical dadoes $^{3}\!/_{4}$" wide x $^{1}\!/_{8}$" deep on both sides of the jig for a $^{3}\!/_{4}$" x 1¼" x 18" long fence. This allows you to flip the fence and cut slots in the opposite upright.
5. Set up the router with a $^{5}\!/_{8}$" dovetail bit and a $^{5}\!/_{8}$" guide bushing, and set the depth of cut to $^{3}\!/_{8}$" deep.
6. Rout through the fence. Use the width of the routed slot when laying out the rungs.

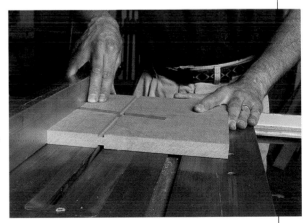

Cut the shallow dadoes on both sides of the jig for a fence to align the jig on the ladder side.

Cut the slots in the sliding dovetail jig to width on the table saw with the miter gauge set at the proper angle.

Photo B: Clamp the two sides of the ladder together to lay out the rung locations.

4. Cut off the bottoms of the ladder uprights so they will stand on the floor at the proper angle.

5. Reset the bevel gauge to the angle for the upper faces of the ladder that will rest against the side rail.

6. Mark this angle out on the top of the uprights.

7. Cut the tops of the uprights to length and to shape on the bandsaw.

8. Sand the rounded shape smooth, and plane the angled faces flat and straight. Check to be sure that the top of the ladder is flush with the top of the side rail when it's angled the proper amount.

Routing the ladder uprights for the rungs

I use sliding dovetails to fasten the rungs to the ladder. You could choose a simpler method using dadoes or cleats. Either will require the addition of some hardware (screws or bolts) to reinforce the joint.

Photo C: The stopped-dovetail-slot jig is set for cutting. To the left of the jig is the slot just routed.

Photo D: Rout the dovetails in the ends of the rungs on the router table with a high fence. Use a large square of plywood as a guide and push stick.

BUNK BED SAFETY

Bunk beds can be dangerous for kids. To help make them less so, there are fairly specific guidelines from the American Society for Testing and Materials (ASTM) and the Consumer Product Safety Commission that you should follow.

The safety guidelines for bunk beds boil down to the following:

- There should be no open spaces greater than 3½ in. either between the guardrail and bed frame or in the headboard and footboard on the top bunk.
- Guardrails should be located on both sides of the top bunk to prevent a child from slipping between the bed and the wall.

- The mattress support must be secure, to eliminate the possibility of the upper bed falling through onto the lower bed.

There are a few other safety suggestions that you should pay attention to as well. Make sure there is at least 5 in. from the top of the mattress to the top of the guardrails. Check from time to time to be sure that the bed bolts and ladder fasteners are secure. Put a nightlight in the room to make it easier for the child on the top bunk to get down if necessary. Make sure that children realize that bunk beds can be dangerous and they must follow rules when using them. The beds are neither a climbing gym nor a trampoline, and you should strongly discourage them from being used as either.

1. Make a router jig to guide the dovetail slot cuts in the ladder uprights (see "Jig for Routing Dovetail Slots"on p. 175).

2. Lay both uprights together, back edge to back edge (the back is the side toward the bed), and mark both the top and bottom of each rung on the inside faces.

3. Mark the dovetail slot locations centered between the rung lines. The opening in the fence on the jig indicates what size slots to mark (see **photo B** on p. 176).

4. Secure the fence in the jig, and lay the jig on an upright so the slot will be parallel to the angled bottom of the upright.

5. Align the opening on the jig's fence with the marks on the upright and rout the slot (see **photo C** on p. 176).

6. When you're done with one upright, remove the fence from the jig, and switch it over to the other side. Flip the jig over, and rout all of the dovetail slots in the other side.

Making and fitting the rungs

1. Cut the rungs to length.

2. Set up a router table with the same dovetail bit you used to rout the slots in the uprights.

Photo E: Commercial bed-rail fasteners make the perfect ladder joint.

3. Install a high fence on the router table with an opening for the bit.

4. Set the bit depth to give you a dovetail equal in length to the depth of the slot. Then set the fence so that just a small amount of the router bit is exposed.

5. Make a test cut on the end of a scrap piece of rung stock, using a large square of plywood or MDF as a guide for pushing. The guide will support the rung at 90 degrees to the table and will also help keep your hands out of the way.

6. Adjust the fence until you have a dovetail that fits tightly into the dovetail slots in the uprights, and rout all of the ends of the rungs (see **photo D** on p. 177).

7. When you've cut all of the rungs, reset the fence a little deeper so you can rout away the front edge of the dovetails to fit in the stopped dovetail groove by flipping the rung 90 degrees in the cut so the edge instead of the side is against the fence.

8. Test the dovetails in their grooves, and if they fit, glue them into place.

9. Plane the back edges flush after the glue is dry.

Attaching the ladder to the bed

How you attach the ladder depends on whether your bunk beds will come apart or not. I used commercial bed-rail fasteners to attach the ladder to my one-piece bunk (see **photo E**). I know it's a little quirky, but it's a perfect use for this hook-and-slot type of fastener. You could just screw the ladder into place from inside the rail if you prefer a simpler solution.

1. Scribe the shallow mortise locations for the fasteners carefully, then rout away most of the waste with a $1/8$-in. straight bit.

2. Pare to the lines with the chisel and check the fit of the plate.

3. Mark out the locations for the pilot holes for the screws as well as the locations for the deeper recesses needed to accommodate any extra metal on the back of the hooks.

4. On the bed rail side of the joint, rout away room for the hooks to lock down through the slots. Note that the slotted half of the hardware is asymmetrical and only works with the correct end up (slots closer to the top). Otherwise, the screws get in the way.

5. Screw the hardware into place and check the fit. To tighten the joint between the ladder and the rail, you can try setting the slotted half of the hardware slightly deeper into the rail.

FINISHING UP

The only quirk in finishing this bed is that the rungs on the ladder shouldn't be too slippery. I used the same oil and wax finish as on the rest of the bed (see Appendix on p. 182 for finishing suggestions), but sanded the tops of the rungs only up to 120 grit. I then finished them with oil, but without the usual wet sanding up to 400 grit. I did not wax the rungs either. To do so would invite a slip and a fall.

Tip: The secret to a good fit with a sliding dovetail joint is lots of test cuts. Make sure you have some extra rung stock so you can cut as many test joints as you need.

Bunk Bed/Twin Bed Conversion

One of the more interesting design options for bunk beds is to make them knock down into two twin-size beds. You use the bottom bed headboard and footboard as the headboards for both twin beds, and use the top bed headboard and footboard as the footboards. For stacking,

you'll need to drill a few extra holes in the legs so the bunk beds can key together with metal rods (don't use a wooden dowel). You can add a plug or finial to the tops of the legs on the bottom bed to cover the holes for these rods in a decorative way when the beds are apart.

STACKED

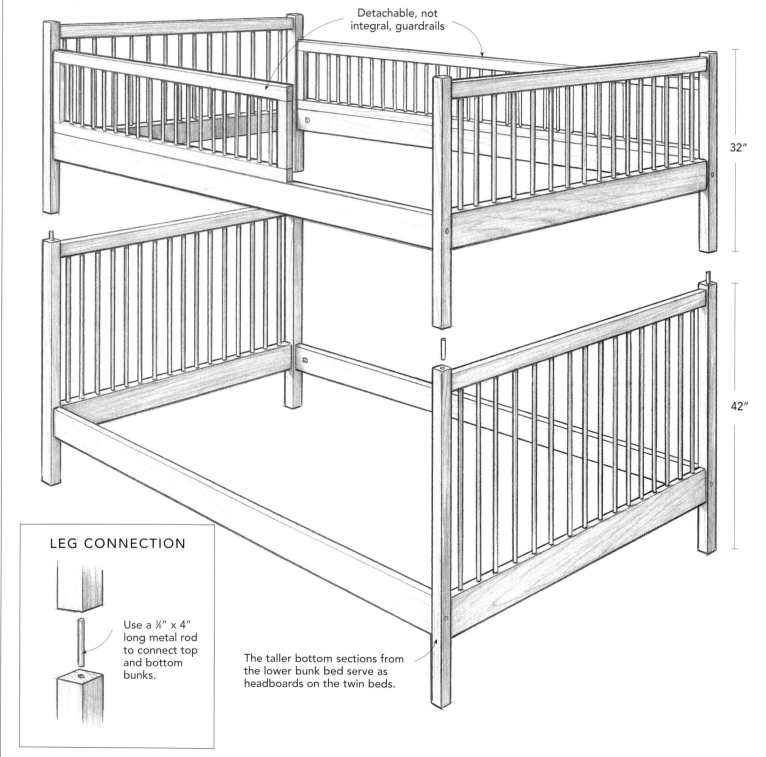

Detachable, not integral, guardrails

32"

42"

LEG CONNECTION

Use a ⅜" x 4" long metal rod to connect top and bottom bunks.

The taller bottom sections from the lower bunk bed serve as headboards on the twin beds.

TWO TWIN BEDS

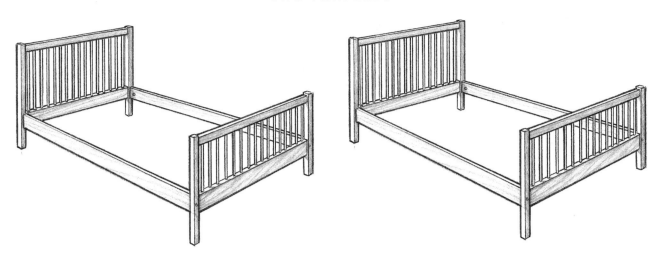

MAKING A LADDER HOOK

If you're making beds that come apart, you won't want hardware or holes in the side rails for attaching the ladder. You can buy ladder hangers from some woodworking-supply catalogs. Unfortunately, the hangers I found work with ¾-in.-thick side rails but not with the 1⁵⁄₁₆-in.-thick rails I use for this bed.

You can make your own hangers pretty easily by bending ⅛-in.-thick by ¾-in.-wide aluminum bar stock with the help of a metalworking vise. I used a block of wood the same thickness as the bed rail to help bend the metal to its proper shape. Cut the hangers to size and drill them for the screws that attach to the ladder and to the inside of the rail. You may want to rout a recess in the angled face of the ladder to conceal the hook. The top will still be exposed.

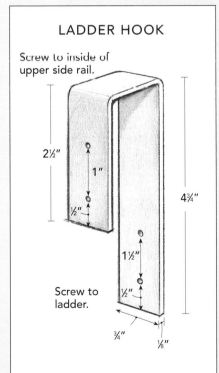

LADDER HOOK

Screw to inside of upper side rail.

2½"

1"

½"

4¾"

1½"

Screw to ladder.

½"

¾"

⅛"

To bend the ladder hook to shape, use a piece of scrap the same thickness as the rail for a form. Another piece of straight scrap helps you keep the back of the hook flat.

APPENDIX: FINISHING BEDS WITH OIL AND WAX

THE FINISH THAT I generally apply to my beds is a thinned oil and varnish blend commonly known as Danish oil. After it cures, I apply a thin coat of wax. It's easy to apply with no special equipment. The finish is less resistant to water and staining than a lacquer finish (which isn't usually a problem on beds anyhow) but is much easier to maintain. You see and feel the wood surface, not a film over it. An oil and wax finish is usually not as formal-looking as lacquer, but it still makes a beautiful and rich finish.

Surface Preparation

Before you start, you should examine the bed carefully for any defects: scratches, dents, planer marks, glue spots, or anything else that might happen to it in the course of sitting around in your shop. Fix these defects before you apply the finish. Although you will be able to work on problems later, it will take some extra effort. Sand everything to 180 or 220 grit. Leave no visible swirl marks.

Three Coats over Three Days

For safety, you should wear gloves when finishing and work in a well-ventilated area and/or wear a respirator with an organic compounds filter.

1. Apply the first coat of oil with a small piece of rag. Get the wood evenly wet; be generous with the oil. Most of this will probably be absorbed into the wood quite rapidly. Rewet the entire surface with more oil. Let the oil soak in for about 15 minutes, then wipe it off thoroughly with a clean rag. Pay particular attention to where pieces join together since it is harder to wipe there. Let the bed sit overnight to dry. Dispose of all oily rags carefully. They can spontaneously combust.

2. Sand the second coat of oil into the wood. Start by applying a good soaking coat with a rag, as with the first coat. Then wet-sand with 320-grit wet-or-dry sandpaper, sanding only with (in the direction of) the grain. Put a little oil on the sandpaper as well. Wipe off after a few minutes—sooner than with the first coat. Again, let the bed sit overnight to dry.

3. The third coat is sanded just like the second coat, with 400-grit wet-or-dry sandpaper. After you've wiped the piece off, let it sit for a half hour or so, and then wipe it down again with a clean rag. Depending on the wood, you may have to wipe the piece a few more times if the oil comes back to the surface. Again, pay particular attention to the joints and other hard-to-wipe places. Any oil left on the surface will turn gummy and will be harder to deal with once dry. Let the bed sit overnight to dry. If the oil continues to "bleed" out of the pores, you should delay waxing until this stops.

Wax the piece with a good furniture-quality paste wax. Apply just a little bit of wax at a time with a pad of 0000 steel wool (extra fine), rubbing it in well with the grain. Be fairly stingy with the wax. You want some on the piece but not much. And what you put on should be evenly applied. Buff with a soft cloth. You may need to go back with a clean pad of steel wool or a fine plastic abrasive pad, such as Scotch-Brite, and rub the finish again to even it out. The result should be very smooth and lustrous.

Maintaining the Finish

To clean or dust the wood, I use a few drops of lemon oil on a rag. (The same oily rag disposal precautions apply here, too.) The lemon oil really doesn't do much more than clean, however. To restore the finish if the piece is damaged or is just looking dry, oil once again with Danish oil, wiping dry carefully. Wax if you find it necessary to restore the luster and the feel of the freshly finished piece.

SOURCES

Bed Hardware

There are many sources for bed hardware. Most of the major woodworking supply catalogs carry bed bolts and a few other items. The following have a greater variety of hardware and may have some higher quality items as well.

WHITECHAPEL, LTD.
P.O. Box 136
Wilson, WY 83014
(800) 468-5534
Beautiful bed bolt covers, bed bolts and wrenches, mattress hanger irons, and other bed fasteners

HORTON BRASSES
P.O. Box 95
Cromwell, CT 06416
(203) 635-4400
Bed bolts and covers, mattress hanger irons

LEE VALLEY TOOLS
P.O. Box 1780
Ogdensburg, NY 13669
(800) 871-8158
Barrel nuts and bolts (listed as bed hardware and also as workbench bolts)

ROCKLER (formerly Woodworkers' Store)
4365 Willow Dr.
Medina, MN 55340
(800) 279-4441
All sorts of bed hardware, table corner brackets

Dowels

MIDWEST DOWEL WORKS
4631 Hutchinson Rd.
Cincinnati, OH 45248
(800) 555-0133

METRIC CONVERSION CHART

INCHES	CENTIMETERS	MILLIMETERS	INCHES	CENTIMETERS	MILLIMETERS
⅛	0.3	3	13	33.0	330
¼	0.6	6	14	35.6	356
⅜	1.0	10	15	38.1	381
½	1.3	13	16	40.6	406
⅝	1.6	16	17	43.2	432
¾	1.9	19	18	45.7	457
⅞	2.2	22	19	48.3	483
1	2.5	25	20	50.8	508
1¼	3.2	32	21	53.3	533
1½	3.8	38	22	55.9	559
1¾	4.4	44	23	58.4	584
2	5.1	51	24	61.0	610
2½	6.4	64	25	63.5	635
3	7.6	76	26	66.0	660
3½	8.9	89	27	68.6	686
4	10.2	102	28	71.1	711
4½	11.4	114	29	73.7	737
5	12.7	127	30	76.2	762
6	15.2	152	31	78.7	787
7	17.8	1/8	32	81.3	813
8	20.3	203	33	83.8	838
9	22.9	229	34	86.4	864
10	25.4	254	35	88.9	889
11	27.9	279	36	91.4	914
12	30.5	305			

INDEX

INDEX